JOE LISTER: MASTER BUILDER

ROBERT INGLE

Published by
TG Publishing
17 Marcliff Crescent
Listerdale
Rotherham
S66 2AU
tg@rombooks.co.uk

By the same author:

THOMAS COOK OF LEICESTER

JOE LISTER: Master Builder
First published in 2007
by TG Publishing

ISBN: 978-0-955574-20-7

Printed by Raphael Design Ltd.
Typeset in Century Schoolbook.
www.raphaeldesign.co.uk

In memory

of

Gilian

who provided the inspiration for this biography of her
remarkable grandfather

ACKNOWLEDGMENTS

I am extremely grateful to the family of Joe Lister – his daughter, Marjorie, and his granddaughters, Gilian and Jane – for their invitation to undertake this project and for allowing me unlimited access to his surviving letters and papers. I also owe many thanks to Malcolm Leader whose knowledge of the history of Joe's imposing residence, Castle House, Listerdale, is unsurpassed. Joe Lister's nephew, Ian, has also provided valuable information on life in Castle House in the 1930s and 40s. Jill Hamilton, herself the author of many books, has given me great help and encouragement as well as providing very constructive criticism. Dorothy Havenhand gave me some very useful information via the Rotherham Family History Society on the ancestry of Joe Lister. David Gray has been an excellent source of advice on the intricacies of word processing and computers, thereby rendering the task of producing the text and illustrations much easier. I am also indebted to Penny Draper for her work in early proof-reading and her suggestions for improving the text as well as her valuable work in compiling the index. Arthur Cowling provided very useful information on Joe Lister's friendship with his father, Dick Cowling, the Coxswain of the Flamborough Lifeboat in the 1930s, and kindly gave me permission to reproduce the photograph of his father pictured on page 165. The Veteran Car Club of Great Britain were most helpful in providing information on the 1914 Sabella, one of Joe's early cars, and I am also grateful to Rotherham Public Libraries for their assistance with my research into the local newspapers. Colin Cook gave very valuable advice in my attempts to unravel Joe's enigmatic motto, *Une seule me suffit*, carried on the coat of arms which appears in the window of Castle House.

A great many others have offered invaluable help by giving me their own personal memories and anecdotes of Joe Lister and Listerdale from its early development until Joe's untimely death in 1947.

Finally, I should like to thank my wife, Sue, who also played a very important part in encouraging me to take on the project and who has endured without complaint those long periods when I was out of all communication with her whilst being deeply engrossed in the researching and preparing of the text. Any errors contained herein are entirely my responsibility.

Robert Ingle,
Leicester,
January, 2007.

CONTENTS

ILLUSTRATIONS

INTRODUCTION

It was a chance meeting on a cold Saturday morning early in 1921 that led to the creation of Listerdale, a large estate of houses on the outskirts of Rotherham in South Yorkshire. Two men were to be seen in conversation standing on a 'rough hill-top' near some old quarries in The Brecks, at the time an area of farmland just outside Rotherham Borough. The following chapters tell the personal journey of one of those involved, Joseph Charles Lister, tracing his story from humble beginnings in a small semi-detached house in Rotherham to a newly built nineteen room castellated property complete with landscaped grounds and terraces. Joe was no ordinary character and was renowned in later life for being a colourful eccentric. He was the 'Sealed Letter Man' who left unopened any letters he received and always walked about with his bootlaces untied. Joe's explanation for this peculiarity was startlingly simple. A doctor had once told him, he claimed, that he would die with his boots on, leading him to reason that should he in any circumstances ever find himself in mortal danger he could kick off the untied boots in the nick of time, cheat death and maybe the doctor. Perhaps a more down to earth explanation was that, knowing of Joe's passion for cars (he bought well over 80 during his lifetime and then gave some of them away) coupled with his well-known reckless manner of driving, the doctor had simply foretold that Joe would most probably die in a road crash. He did not, as it happens, despite being involved in numerous car accidents, some of which were quite serious.

Starting as a lowly clerk in a firm of local timber merchants, Joe was a hard-working young man who eventually began an enterprising gamble when he was approaching the age of 40. As the 19th century drew to a close, his grandfather, 'Old Joe' Lister, had built houses and then attempted to sell them to working people; alas for 'Old Joe', his altruistic vision did not wholly succeed, despite evidence of his considerable building activity still to be seen in Rotherham. Too many people were still too poor to be able to buy their homes on his instalment plan and eventually the scheme had to be abandoned, but the grandson began his own building career some years later by reviving the same idea of building houses for sale to owner occupiers. Like his grandfather before him, it began well and he built what is now known as 'Old Listerdale' which was advertised to prospective purchasers as a 'perfect little arcadia'. But after this initial success and like his forbear, he abandoned the scheme, then he boldly changed direction going much further than his grandfather, borrowed huge amounts of capital in the depth of one of the most severe economic slumps in history and used it to create an estate of houses for rent.

Joe Lister became the builder of his housing estate almost by accident and certainly never began with an ambition to build and own 650 houses. He was a rare character who at his funeral was described as 'the most talked of man in South Yorkshire', an individualist 'coming straight from the pages of Elizabethan history', and his impact on the life of the whole area was significant with his name living on in the locality – Listerdale – on the eastern edges of Rotherham. The estate might be small in comparison with many of the council estates that now cover much of Britain's townscapes and cannot be compared to the great ducal estates of Grosvenor and Bedford in London, but when completed by Joe in the 1930s it became one of the largest privately owned residential estates outside London and it remains so to this day. Although 250 houses have been sold over the years to meet tax demands, 400 rented houses still form part of Listerdale Estates and over 80 years after it all began it is still in private hands.

Landlords have certainly not occupied a very affectionate place in popular English mythology, in spite of the fact that (or perhaps because of it) so many people were once dependent on them. Even as late as 1938, despite the growth of council estates, 57 per cent of all houses in Britain were owned by private landlords. Joe Lister, the eccentric buccaneer, became a landlord who refused to fit any stereotype and who, at his own enormous risk, provided decent, affordable homes for many families. He was no absentee landlord but lived on the estate and was greatly involved with the welfare of his tenants.

Joe was an audacious and controversial character. His no-nonsense approach led to many fiercely contested battles with the local authorities both before and after the estate was built. He eventually conceived the idea of a complete and self-contained 'garden suburb' (with plans for an early version of 'on-line' shopping) but it was never fully realised, curtailed by a shortage of capital, the outbreak of war in 1939 and his own early death from cancer at the age of 61 in 1947. It was, though, his dogged determination, his willingness to risk everything and his sheer effort which culminated in the creation of the Listerdale housing estate that can be seen today on the outskirts of Rotherham, complete with the adjacent open spaces that he purchased and set aside for the enjoyment of his tenants.

PART ONE: SOLID FOUNDATIONS

CHAPTER ONE:

THE LISTERS OF ROTHERHAM

Joseph Charles Lister was born in Rotherham on October 27th, 1885, the first son of James and Ada Lister. As the infant Joe gradually became aware of his immediate surroundings he could hardly fail to see solid reminders of his family heritage for its prosperity depended on the local building trade, and to understand anything of the complexities of the subsequent life and career of Joseph Lister it is necessary to look in some detail at this important family influence on his young life; the very existence of the house he lived in as a child and most of its neighbours was the direct result of his family's involvement in the construction industry. The Lister family had created the neighbourhood. This enterprise, although in his childhood Joe could not have realised it, was of no ordinary character for the family were engaged in a pioneering venture which, in the 1880s, was many years ahead of its time, and in later life Joe was to refer back to it on several occasions as the source of much of his own inspiration. In the days when many people had to struggle to afford the rent for a suitable house in which to live and bring up a family, the Lister enterprise in the last quarter of the 19th century was an audacious attempt to transform tenants into property owners and they went about it using all the marketing techniques available to them at that time.

'WORKING MEN – BECOME YOUR OWN LANDLORDS!' was the striking headline of the leaflet that circulated in the cramped streets of late Victorian Rotherham, an industrial town in what was then the West Riding of Yorkshire. The year was 1889 and the leaflet set out in detail how a 'Freehold House & Garden' could be purchased by the occupier on 'easy terms' in 14 years. The cost of the house was £140 and the interest on the loan was to be charged at 5% per annum. By paying £14 per year on what would now be called a repayment mortgage the house could be completely paid for by the end of the fourteenth year (with a little extra to be paid in that year to clear the outstanding balance). Particulars of this interesting scheme could be obtained from 'J. LISTER, Oxford Street, Rotherham'.

Although the Lister family claim to have been settled in the area since the 17th century, the author of the leaflet is the first of them about whom there is any real knowledge. Born in Conisborough, Yorkshire, in 1828, he is known in the family as 'Old Joe' and he was the grandfather of Joe Lister of Listerdale, the master builder, who was named after him. The only surviving photograph shows 'Old Joe' as a craggy-faced patriarch who would not have looked out of place among the frontiersmen of the expanding United States of America. He was a builder by trade and was responsible for building several streets of housing in the Clifton Park and Eastwood areas of Rotherham in the 1880s, at that time on the edge of the town. One of them, Lister Street, takes its name from him. Walking down this street and the neighbouring Oxford and Cambridge Streets, reputedly named after the Boat Race, the effects of 'Old

'Old Joe' Lister

Joe's' work can still be seen today. Whereas so many of the streets laid out in English cities in the 1880s and 1890s present a solid cliff-wall of terraced housing, these thoroughfares are still notable for their sense of space as they were built at a far lower density than was normal for Victorian working class housing (usually about 40 houses to the acre). There are a few terraces consisting of four or five houses each but it is striking how many of the houses were built as semi-detached, something that was not all that common for artisan dwellings in the last quarter of the 19th century. It reflects 'Old Joe's' pioneering scheme of building to sell to owner-occupiers. The houses are small, plain brick-built dwellings with square front bays and each pair stands as a foursquare block with very little decoration on the outside. They each have a side door as the main entrance, a long front garden, and all are approached by a drive, an almost unheard of feature of houses built for the Victorian working classes. 'Old Joe' had carefully worked out for the benefit of the public how his house-purchase scheme could be afforded by detailing the payments and balances throughout each of the years of the loan and then pointing out that renting a similar house would cost a tenant £9 a year anyway, a figure which he claimed should be set against the purchase payments. By this calculation, a £140 house would only really have 'cost' the purchaser a total of just over £70 by the end of the loan period.

'Old Joe' was a pioneer and could claim to be the first local builder who set out to make it possible for a working man to buy the house he lived in. With average wages in the Rotherham area in 1889 at about £50 a year, the scheme could just have been afforded by people in steady work and on such an income. Owner occupation was not completely unknown, as building societies, set up on co-operative lines, had been operating for more than a century. It was not, however, really part of the culture of 19th century Britain. There was always the risk of loss of work through sickness or unemployment and there was simply no protection such as statutory sickness benefit or unemployment pay which only began in 1909. The outcome facing those who could not keep up the instalments on any house purchase could have easily been eviction and homelessness or the horrors of the workhouse; the part-purchased property would have been repossessed – a situation worse even than being evicted from a rented property – and 'Old Joe's' far sighted scheme was too much ahead of its time, needing a higher standard of living for most people to enable them to afford to take the risk. It was not taken up in great enough numbers and had to be abandoned. But it was never forgotten by his family.

'Old Joe' Lister had not always been employed in the building trade and when he was 25, he had married Jane Jackson, the daughter of a farmer, from Wath, Yorkshire, in the Parish Church of Sheffield, now Sheffield Cathedral, on November 19th, 1853. The new Mrs. Lister was 28 at the time of their marriage. 'Old Joe' is described on the marriage certificate as a 'Wharfinger' (a description no longer used but which meant the owner of a wharf and no doubt referring to the canal trade that went on in that part of Yorkshire). The name of Joseph appears to have been a family tradition for 'Old Joe' was the son of another Joseph Lister who is described as a 'Carpenter'. The choice of Sheffield Parish Church is curious for neither of them came from the town, except that they appear to have been living there at the time, and at the same address, given on the marriage certificate as 'South St. Park'. On 27th June, 1859, a son, James, was born. The Listers must have been reasonably prosperous for, at a time when most children could not attend school, James Lister was first sent to the 'British School', a nonconformist institution which provided a rudimentary education in Rawmarsh Road, Rotherham, and later he took up a place at the 'Ellis Boarding School', eight miles away to the south-east at Roche Abbey. His formal education was completed when he enrolled as a student at the Mechanics Institute in Rotherham.

James Lister

James became a builder like his father and one of his early positions was serving as Clerk of the Works during the alterations to the Rotherham Poor Law Institution (the Rotherham Workhouse) in Alma Road, Rotherham. In the 1901 census he is still described as being a 'Clerk of Works to Builder' but by then he had actually risen to hold the position of Estate Agent for the Rother Vale Collieries Company Ltd, a post he held until his death in 1932 at the age of 73.

In 1902 this particular mining company decided to sink a new colliery at Thurcroft, a village a few miles east of Rotherham, and James was put in charge of constructing the housing estate to provide homes for the miners who were to work at the colliery. 'Old Joe' had been in the vanguard of new thinking regarding home ownership and his son, James, was now about to put into practice some of the latest 'state of the art' thinking concerning housing design and estate lay-out. The work of both father and son foreshadowed the even greater achievement of the grandson - the creation of the large housing estate at Listerdale.

When James Lister was handed the task of designing the colliery housing estate it coincided with a period of intense debate over what should constitute the ideal housing development; it was a time when the idea of 'garden cities' was beginning to gain popularity. Bedford Park, at Chiswick in London, although more a 'garden suburb' of semi-detached villas for the middle classes than a complete 'garden city', was begun in 1875 and Ebenezer Howard, generally recognised as the founder of the garden city movement, published *Tomorrow: A Peaceful Path to Real Reform* in 1898. It was later republished in 1902 under the title, *Garden Cities of Tomorrow*. The background to Howard's thinking was the rapid growth of Victorian cities as industrialisation and population growth had attracted more and more people into the expanding towns in search of better employment and higher wages. When the Victorian Age opened in 1837 there were only 5 cities with populations of more than 100,000; by 1891 there were 22. In 1801 only three out of ten people lived in urban areas; by 1911 that figure had increased to eight in ten. Adequate housing provision had not kept up with this vast expansion of industrial towns that followed the increasing demand for labour to operate the new factories. Factory owners had often employed speculative builders to construct rows of sub-standard and high-density housing in close proximity to the factories, with the predictable results of overcrowding, poor sanitation and disease. The frequent outbreaks of cholera between 1831 and 1854 which killed many thousands of people were remembered with horror and there was widespread concern for the health of the nation, so much so that 'the condition of the people', a phrase coined by Thomas Carlyle in a pamphlet published in 1839, became a question of frequent political debate. Housing was to occupy an important part in that debate for a long time and the Lister family was eventually to play its part in the measures that were taken to resolve an acute social problem. The broader scene was gradually being set for the achievement of the third generation of the family at Listerdale. Howard, whose ideas had matured after his involvement in the rebuilding of Chicago after the disastrous fire there in 1871, came to the conclusion that future developments needed to be planned with fresh air and green spaces in mind.

The building of the first complete 'garden city' began at Letchworth in 1903 but there were earlier examples of self-contained industrial villages based on 'garden city' lines. William Lever, who made a fortune out of Sunlight Soap, built a model village, Port Sunlight, on the banks of the Mersey in 1888 to house his factory workers; George Cadbury began building Bourneville, just outside Birmingham, in 1894. His development was different from that of Lever's in that he made half of the houses available to the general public. The debate is still continuing as to whether these industrial pioneers of better housing for workers were motivated by philanthropy or had simply realised that better housed operatives become more efficient producers. Whatever the motives, many families certainly benefited as a result.

It is not known how much James Lister may have studied the garden city movement of Howard and others, but in 1932 his obituary in the *Rotherham Advertiser* referred to him in its headline as the 'Architect of Model Colliery Housing Estate' and stated, 'When the colliery at Thurcroft was sunk he devised the lay-out of the colliery company's housing estate on model lines. This was one of the first colliery 'garden cities' in England, and it attracted such widespread attention that in the early part of 1914 – before the European War broke out – a number of German industrialists came over specially to view it.'

In the Parish Church of Rotherham on 13th December, 1883, James Lister, the 'practical son of a practical builder', had married Ada Rylance Shutt who came from nearby Sheffield. It is intriguing that the wedding did not take place in Sheffield near the bride's home and could indicate that the Lister family was more established as a local family who could cope with the financial and social demands of a wedding celebration. He was 24 at the time of their marriage and Ada was 25. Her father, James Shutt, is described as an 'Engine Tenter', a description which could imply that he looked after a locomotive on the railways or, more likely, that he was responsible for looking after the steam-engine which drove the machinery in a factory. It does not appear to have been a highly skilled job and it would involve stoking the engine and maintaining the supply of water to its boiler. Ada, who in the 1881 census is referred to as a 'Shop Waitress', is simply described as a 'spinster' on the marriage certificate, while James Lister is described as a 'joiner' and it is interesting to note that his son, Joe Lister of Listerdale, also in his turn began his working life in the timber trade before becoming, like his father, a builder.

Ada Lister travelling in style in one of Joe's early cars, a Clement Talbot

James Lister became well thought of in Rotherham and the obituary notice describes him '...as much respected as known. Unobtrusive in manner, he never sought public office, the only semi-public post he held being that of a director of the First Public Thrift Building Society, of which he was one of the founders.' Ada was his complete opposite in many ways. A remarkable woman for mid-Victorian England, she actively involved herself in public life as well as bringing up their six children; she appears in the family photographs as a very determined and formidable looking lady and gives the impression that she would stand no nonsense. She came from a nonconformist background and in politics she supported the Liberal party of William Gladstone who was well into his second ministry at the time she married James Lister.

In the 1885 general election, Ada campaigned for the Liberal candidate for Rotherham, A.H.D.Acland, and became one of the first presidents of the Rotherham Women's Liberal Association. She would be greatly involved in running the committee rooms whereby the party workers could keep track of their supporters and ensure that they turned out to vote. Acland was successful and was appointed by Gladstone to a post in government. He became President of the Council for Education, an early forerunner of the Department of Education, and Ada would, through her political activities, now have some access to a far wider world than provincial Rotherham. James followed his wife's Liberalism and was a member of the Rotherham Liberal Federation but, after her death from cancer at the end of January, 1924, he subsequently changed allegiance and joined the Conservative Club.

Ada also joined in the movement to promote the cause of temperance. This was a very widespread and popular campaign at the time which had gathered momentum after the Beerhouse Act of 1830 had reached the statute book. It was a well-intentioned Act designed to encourage the population away from cheap home-produced gin, 'mother's ruin', but it only succeeded in adding to the problem as under its provisions, anyone could open a 'public house' for the sale of beer, but not spirits, on application to the excise authorities and the payment of a licence fee.   Over 30,000 of these new beerhouses were opened within a short time of the passing of the Act but the population still continued to drink gin as well as drinking more beer. Not for the last time, drunkenness was seen as a major cause of many of the social evils of the time and George Sims, the social reformer, had commented that 'Drink gave the poor the Dutch courage they needed to go on living'.   The Victorians were always obsessed with classification and they even classified the poor into the 'deserving' and the 'undeserving'.   Poverty exacerbated by hard drinking would certainly put anyone into the 'undeserving' category and even if the bottom was reached and the only place of shelter remained the workhouse, the division continued, even in those grim buildings.

Temperance, or even total abstinence, was propagated as the best way to become 'deserving' and every town of any size eventually had its Temperance Association and sometimes its Temperance Hall where 'rational', i.e. alcohol-free, entertainments would take place to encourage people away from the beerhouses and the gin-palaces.   The temperance movement had begun in Preston in Lancashire in 1835 when a local cheese-maker, Joseph Livesey, had persuaded a small group of men in the town to sign a pledge of temperance and the British Association for the Promotion of Temperance was born. It gathered momentum and was later taken up by the Churches, particularly the nonconformist ones.   Ada was successful in her involvement with temperance and eventually rose to become President of the British Women's Temperance Association where she was now in excellent company following in the footsteps of Rosalind, Lady Carlisle, who was elected President of the Women's Temperance Association after first attending a local meeting of the Temperance Association in 1881. She was the formidable wife of George Howard, 9th Earl of Carlisle, of Castle Howard, and used her influence and position to close down public houses or convert them into coffee houses or temperance hotels but Ada, for all her obvious determination, is not recorded as succeeding in closing any licensed premises in Rotherham.

Many years later, in 1913, Ada became directly involved in local politics. It is widely believed that no woman could vote or stand as a candidate for office until 1918 and in parliamentary elections this was perfectly true but it did not apply to local government. The test there was not so much gender but the payment of local rates and Ada Lister obviously met that test or she would not have been eligible to stand. Local government in the late 19th and early 20th centuries consisted of elected councils and separately elected Boards of Guardians whose responsibility was to administer the welfare of the poor of the locality in accordance with the Poor Law Amendment Act of 1834. In effect it meant acting as governors of the union workhouses that were created by that Act. Ada turned her attention in that direction and in April, 1913, stood as a candidate for the Board of Guardians, not this time as a Liberal but in the interests of the Rotherham Ratepayers' Association and her election address is notable for its economy with words. Claiming 'to know something about the needs of the people' in the East Ward where she had lived for 30 years, she simply promises that, if elected, she will do her best 'to help in administering justice with economy'. Her attempt was successful and she was duly elected to the Board, one of its first women members, and served until 1922 when she decided not to seek re-election, almost certainly on the grounds of her failing health. Her particular interest was the plight of poor women and children and, although she was never a suffragette, she was intensely interested in women's rights at a time when a woman's involvement with public affairs was much frowned upon.

Ada Lister's Election Leaflet

What effect his wife's activities had upon the more reserved James Lister is not known but it was against this background that Joe Lister and his five brothers and sisters were brought up. Joe appears to have inherited his mother's strong personality along with his father's practical skills. This was a very important inheritance but it was all that James passed on to his eldest son. Joe Lister records in his 1936 account of his life that he had asked his father to leave him nothing in his will 'except a few heirlooms' as his idea was that 'wherever and however' he finished his career he was determined that it was to be of his own making. This did not mean, however, that Joe had no interest in his father's estate who, on his death, owned at least twelve houses in Rotherham which were put up for auction on May 9th, 1932. Joe arranged for his sister, Jessie and his brother, Donald, to buy some of this property to keep it in the family. Later Joe bought out Donald's interest and he later helped him even further by letting him draw the rent of one of the houses on the Listerdale Estate. Like many aspiring Victorian middle-class families, the Lister's philosophy was based on the self-help and self-improvement ideas of Samuel Smiles whose book, entitled *Self-Help*, was published in 1859 and was widely read at the time.

CHAPTER TWO:

AUTUMN'S CHILD

James and Ada had married in the dark days of winter and moved into 52 Oxford Street, Rotherham. It was the Lister family home, one of the semi-detached houses built by 'Old Joe' Lister among the many properties constructed by him in the surrounding streets. Both the Rotherham censuses for 1881 and 1891 reveal that it was also occupied by 'Old Joe' and his wife, Jane. Joseph had by then become very much a family name for nearby, at number 53, lived James' sister, Mrs Hall, with a son, Joseph Lister Hall, who enlisted in the 1914-18 War and was eventually killed at the battle of Ypres in 1915. It would appear from the census returns that James and Ada moved into number 52 with James' parents until they found a house of their own. The 24 year old James would already have been living there but what the forceful and resourceful Ada made of the situation when she moved in as his wife can only be imagined. Much of the running of the house must have fallen to her as there is no record that the Listers had any domestic servants in residence. There may also have been a need for help in looking after the elderly parents. The evidence is that they were sharing the house for over seven years by which time they had at least three children of their own for, as was so often the case with Victorian newly-weds, it was not long before a family began to arrive and within a year after the marriage a daughter, Jane, was born. In later life she became known as 'Jennie' or 'Ginnie'. It was often the custom in Victorian families to name the first boy and girl after grandparents and this was obviously the case with the children of James and Ada Lister as not many months could have passed after the birth of her first child before Ada became pregnant again and on 27th October, 1885, the first son, Joseph Charles, was born. In June, 1936, Joe Lister wrote about those early days, 'At the time of my birth I already had a sister named Jennie, and afterwards successively born were sister Jessie, brother James Granville, brother Gilbert Henry and brother Thomas Donald'. He adds that they were all still living in 1936.

James Lister and his four sons, c. 1926: Joe, Granville, Gilbert and Donald

The England into which Joe Lister was born was enjoying the calm and self-confident autumn of Queen Victoria's long reign. There had been peace for a very long time with the conflagration of the Napoleonic wars seeming a very distant memory and, even though there had been some dangerous little conflicts such as the Crimean War, fought between 1854 and 1856, peace seemed to be the birthright of all the subjects of the British Queen. *Pax Britannica* was the established world order and Britain was approaching her grandest period of imperial power which was to last until the 'lights went out all over Europe' in the Great War of 1914-1918. The Franco-Prussian War of 1870-1, which was to have a profound effect on the history of the 20th century, had caused little disturbance in Britain which, as Bismarck, the first German Chancellor, correctly predicted, had refused to become embroiled in the conflict, seeing it all as a continental problem. The only effect it seemed to have had on the British population was the advice given to those intending to travel to Paris that they should apply to the Foreign Office for a passport (which at the time was not compulsory for travel abroad) to ensure that once in France they were not mistaken for Prussian spies.

Prosperity had gone hand in hand with this time of peace. Not everyone shared in it; those on the margins of society saw little prosperity, but the Lister family undoubtedly did. With unprecedented increases in population the need for new building was unsurpassed. Rotherham's population increased ninefold in the century between 1801 and 1901, from almost 6,500 to 54,000, and much of this increase was due to the growing industrial wealth of the town attracting families into it from the surrounding areas in search of better wages. In 1871, Rotherham had successfully petitioned to become a Municipal Borough with its own local government, although it never came near to achieving the standing of its near neighbour, Sheffield.

Britain was slowly completing its transition from an aristocratic polity towards a democratic system of parliamentary government. The social pressures that had come in the wake of early industrialisation had led directly to the 1832 Great Reform Act which had increased the size of the electorate, but not by very much. Those who, as a result of the growth of industry, were beginning to wield a new economic power, hitherto in the hands of the landed aristocracy, were demanding a greater role in the political nation. 'Old Joe' Lister would undoubtedly have qualified for the vote under the terms of the 1832 Act as he was an owner of freehold property but his son, James, would be forced to wait until he was in his thirties, even after the extension of the franchise to all adult male householders as a result of the 1867 Second Reform Act, as he would not be regarded as a head of household until sometime in the 1890s when he moved into his own house. Their wives would have had no vote in any parliamentary election. James' own son, Joe Lister, would have to wait until 1918 when he was 33 before he could exercise a right to vote.

Rotherham was mentioned in the Domesday Book as 'Rodreham' and there is evidence of past glories to be seen in the town today including the large and imposing parish church of All Saints set on rising ground and dominating the centre of the town; it clearly must have been a place of some importance in medieval times. The town is situated at the confluence of the Rivers Rother and Don and would have been an important crossing place for travellers. The little Chantry Chapel of Our Lady, restored and preserved on the old bridge, is one of only three surviving examples in England (the others are at Wakefield, Yorkshire, and St. Ives in Cambridgeshire) and is an indication of Rotherham's importance as a bridge over the River Don; medieval travellers would be grateful to find such a chapel and so be able to implore the help of Our Lady, as well as St. Christopher, for the safe continuation of their journeys. In the 19th century the chapel was used for a time as a prison and the bridge on which it stands subsequently became known as 'Gaol Bridge'. Controversial alterations to the bridge were proposed by Rotherham County Borough Council in 1924 and the issue became one of the earliest campaigns taken up by Joe Lister. On December 6th of that year the *Rotherham Advertiser* carried a letter from him which complained of the 'mystery' about the proposals and asked, 'If there is nothing that will arouse public resentment in the new proposals why are they being kept so secret'? In a further letter addressed to the editor of the newspaper but undated, he pulls no punches in his defence of preservation and introduces us to his typically forthright style:

> The sickly sentiments referred to in your columns last week when writing about the improvement?? Of Gaol Bridge is the same sickly sentiment that is termed veneration in connection with other subjects, but just why it should be sickly sentiment because it deals with affairs in Rotherham is hard to understand.
>
> If we must always give way to progress let us make a real good job while we are about it and scrap everything today that is not used for the same purpose as originally, or that can be improved upon from present day requirements, then there will be no need in this world for sickly sentiment, or veneration, that causes us to revere and tolerate things and affairs of the past...
>
> To my mind the only people entitled to pass any real opinion on the destruction of the Old Bridge are Rotherham people bred and born, not people who have come to reside here and aren't

satisfied with the place (Rotherham evidently appealed to them more than did their native heath and with all its faults must have been more attractive) to whom my advice is "If they know of a better Ole go to it".

Perhaps Mr Editor you will inform us how many of Rotherham's Aldermen and Councillors that were bred and born here were at the meeting that decided the Old Bridge's fate and how they voted.

Despite all protestations the bridge eventually disappeared as a crossing and now only a portion of it is preserved with the chapel still intact but reached by a pedestrian way. Today's traffic crosses the river by a modern bridge which has been erected a short distance from the ancient one.

The 1852 *Gazetteer and General Directory of Sheffield* referred to Rotherham as being:

...a busy market town on the navigable part of the River Don and [it] has long been celebrated for its iron and steelworks; its noble gothic church; its extensive corn and cattle market; and for the glasshouses, potteries and iron and coal works in its vicinity.

It is more ancient than its neighbour Sheffield. The houses are generally of stone and some of them are handsomely built, but owing to the low situation and the irregularity and narrowness of the streets, the town has rather a dull appearance.

Sheffield may well have become known as the world centre of the cutlery trade with, first, its abundance of water power to drive the grinding wheels (five rivers run into Sheffield) and then, when the age of steam power dawned, its proximity to another vital source of power, coal, to drive the factory and workshop steam engines. Rotherham was also situated close to coal mines and when Horatio Nelson came to face the combined Franco-

Spanish fleet at Trafalgar it was cannons forged in Rotherham by Samuel Walker & Co. which gave the British sailing ships the edge in that decisive battle. Trafalgar ranks alongside Waterloo as one of the key victories that laid the foundations of the growing British power throughout the 19th century. When Joe Lister was born in 1885, British power across the globe was unrivalled and the Golden Jubilee of Queen Victoria in 1887 was a celebration of British might, only to be surpassed by the extravaganza of the Diamond Jubilee in 1897. Could the sun ever set on the British Empire?

The Lister family would have had no first-hand knowledge of Britain's power overseas for, like most people in Rotherham at the time, they never travelled abroad but they would have been highly conscious of it. As literacy steadily increased, most of the population were becoming avid readers of newspapers, keeping up with the exploits of those who were responsible for the expanding British Empire, and the vast majority of the population shared in the unquestioning belief in the triumphalist progress of their most favoured nation. In 1876, a few years before Joe was born, Britain came very close to war with Russia and the music hall song which then became popular and gave a new word to the English language perhaps sums up the prevailing mood of late Victorian Britain,

> We don't want to fight,
> But by Jingo if we do,
> We've got the ships,
> We've got the men,
> We've got the money too.

The uncertainties and doubts of the 20th century would not cloud the mind of the young Joe Lister as he grew up in the industrial city of Rotherham. All around him he would see evidence of progress - new coal mines, vast iron and steel making plants, and the growing housing estates which his family was helping to build. Among his earliest memories would have been discussions on the state of the building trade between his father and his grandfather and he would have inherited the general belief that during the long and glorious reign of the Queen, life in England had become so much better and that there was every reason to believe that such progress would continue into a sunlit future.

CHAPTER THREE:

A WORTHWHILE EDUCATION

The house in Oxford Street must have become very crowded as the third generation of the Lister family began to grow up and although it is not clear when exactly James Lister and his family moved, it was some time in the 1890s that he bought a block of property on the corner of St Anne's Road and Nelson Street and they moved into a semi-detached house of their own, approximately a quarter of a mile from the old Lister home in Oxford Street. It was 27 St Anne's Road, where Joe continued to live until he married in 1914, eventually moving into a flat with a workshop underneath which was built in the garden. Joe's schooling had just begun and he tells us in his 1936 account that, 'I commenced my education at a private school in Eastwood Mount, run by the Misses Gillott, afterwards attending the Council Infants' School, Wellgate. At the time when I was due for promotion to the Boys' School, the St Ann's(sic) Road School was due for opening, and as we were then living in St Ann's Road...I attended there and was the first boy to be entered on the register.' It would have been quite a walk from Oxford Street to Wellgate, nearer the centre of Rotherham, and no doubt Joe was glad of the school, opened in 1893, situated almost opposite in the street where he was now living. The building is still standing, complete with the inscription 'St Anne's Road Boys' School' and its date stone of 1893.

Both the Wellgate Infants' School and St Anne's Road School attended by Joe Lister were known as 'Board' schools, the first English state schools, so named because they were administered by a local Board of Education, the forerunners of the present local education authorities. The schooling Joe experienced at the St Anne's Road School would have been extremely basic. It was little more than simple instruction in how to read and write and how to master rudimentary arithmetical skills. There would also have been great emphasis placed on religious instruction or 'scripture' as it was sometimes called. In the local board schools there was little attempt to encourage the pupils to think for themselves and scant introduction to great literature, music or art. It could never be called a 'liberal' education and was never intended to be. The Act of Parliament which allowed the setting up of such schools, Forster's Education Act of 1870, was a utilitarian answer to the need for the expansion in education that resulted from the rapid growth of industry in Victorian England and its demands for labour. Appeals to the imagination were not considered necessary for the development of the young pupils' minds, many of whose lives, it was assumed by the authorities, would be spent as operatives in factories in tasks that required little creativity or, in the case of many of Rotherham's inhabitants, in the iron and steelworks or the collieries. The English local board school system of the late 19th century did, however, provide firm grounding in the basic building blocks of education and anyone fortunate enough to go on to secondary education, as Joe did, would have been provided with good solid foundations.

Joe's attendance at a school would probably have ended when he left St Anne's Road School had it not been for the Yorkshire West Riding County Council. Rotherham

Municipal Borough did not make any provision for secondary education in the 1890s but there was a well-established grammar school in the town. Rotherham Grammar School was founded in 1483 by one of the town's illustrious sons, Thomas Scott, who later became known as Thomas Rotherham, Lord Chancellor of England during the reign of Edward IV and who was also Archbishop of York from 1480 until he died in 1500 being then placed in an imposing marble tomb in York Minster (he appears in *Richard III* by William Shakespeare). The school (motto *Ne ingrati videamur*, 'Lest we be ungrateful') began life as the College of Jesus and was erected on the site of Thomas Rotherham's birthplace in the centre of medieval Rotherham. The foundation of the Grammar School itself can be traced back to the requirement that the College should accept 'six of the poorer boys of these parts' to be looked after and taught up to the age of eighteen free of charge. The Grammar School was allowed to continue after the upheavals of the Reformation in the 16th century and was placed in the hands of the Feoffees of the Common Lands of Rotherham for about 300 years. In 1890 these Feoffees bought the premises of Rotherham Independent College, which had been built only a few years before in 1876 as a training college for Congregational ministers until it was decided to move the training arrangements to Bradford, and the Grammar School moved in. This building still exists on Moorgate Road and is now the Thomas Rotherham Sixth Form College and is a co-educational establishment; in 1897, however, the school only admitted boys.

Rotherham did not become a county borough until 1902 which meant the West Riding County Council still retained some jurisdiction over the area until then, and when Joe reached the age of 12 in 1898 it was therefore possible for him to be awarded a 'County Minor Scholarship' to the Grammar School. The money for these scholarships came from grants to the County Council from the Exchequer and, with the competition to obtain one being considerable, the fact that Joe was awarded one is a good indication of his aptitude and ability. His application for the scholarship was acknowledged by a postcard from the West Riding County Council dated April 5th, 1898, and signed by W. Vibart Dixon, 'Clerk to the Technical Instruction Committee'. He sat the examination on Saturday, 21st May, 1898, and in due course a letter arrived formally addressed to him and advising that he had been awarded the County Minor Scholarship which was to run for two years, renewable if he 'should prove a meritorious student'. Joe undoubtedly satisfied this test for the award was extended to run for three years.

Grammar schools provided a means of advancement for countless children who came from families of modest means and most of them were able to provide 'Leaving Exhibitions', scholarships to the Universities of Oxford, Cambridge and London, for their brightest pupils. The ethos of such schools was based on the famous public schools which had just undergone a thorough reformation largely as a result of Dr Thomas Arnold's highly successful tenure as Headmaster of Rugby School. Like the public schools, grammar schools had their 'houses' to encourage a team spirit among their students and they were also based on the prefectorial system whereby the senior boys took some responsibility for the discipline and order of the school. Rotherham Grammar School was not a boarding school and all its pupils were day boys, but Joe would have been exposed to a much more 'liberal' education than could be obtained at the schools run by the local School Board, although even at the Grammar School encouragement of the imagination and thinking for oneself would not be high on the list of priorities. The curriculum would be a mixture of the classical and the practical and included religious knowledge, mathematics, English (grammar as well as literature), art, history, geography, science and French. So much of English education in the 19th and early 20th centuries was influenced by the spirit of Mr Gradgrind, the teacher in *Hard Times*, the novel by Charles Dickens, with his constant cry of 'Facts, facts'. He may have been a caricature but not so wide of the mark of the utilitarian philosophy which guided so much of Victorian education.

Joe was an 'assiduous' pupil if not quite a brilliant one and his view of the examination system was made clear in his 1936 account:

> Whilst at school I obtained quite a number of certificates for examinations and left school being the top boy. The result of examinations to my mind is no record of the student's ability, and my experience in after life justifies the opinion then formed that quite a number of the boys who only managed to struggle through, or failed, were equally as good in the long run as the more successful ones, their mentality being one which did not perhaps allow them to reply to examination questions as successfully as might be, although they were capable of doing it.

Despite this somewhat jaundiced view of examinations Joe had certainly done well. He sat two sets of external examinations, one in December, 1899, and the other in December, 1900, obtaining a second class certificate with a distinction in arithmetic in the University of Cambridge Local Examinations. He did not, however, go on to any higher education which would have meant staying on to take examinations at 18 and, although University may well have been considered with a 'Leaving Exhibition', the fact that there were five other children in the family undoubtedly was a factor in his decision to leave school in the summer of 1901, just before his sixteenth birthday. James, his father, whilst on a very respectable salary, would have found it difficult to support his eldest son through another two years at the Grammar School followed by three years at university, and what of the other boys in the family? It was not generally expected, in 1900, for girls to go on to university but both James Granville and Thomas Donald would have had just cause for grievance if their brother, Joseph Charles, was favoured over them had they harboured any desire to attend university. In any case, in 1900 and for a long time to come after that, universities, particularly Oxford and Cambridge, were dominated by public school entrants who gave the impression of sailing through life with 'effortless superiority'. It is difficult to see Joe, the son of a Rotherham builder and with no land or wealth at the time, flourishing in those social surroundings. In the event, Joe's education did not come to a complete halt when he left the Grammar School for in the early years of his employment he attended 'night school' and obtained certificates in mathematics and, very significantly, in building construction.

CHAPTER FOUR:

HE STOOPS TO CONQUER

When Joe left the Grammar School in the middle of 1901 the Victorian Age had officially just come to an end. The Queen had died the previous January and her son, 'Bertie', the Prince of Wales, acceded to the throne as Edward VII but little change would have been noticed by anyone living at the time. The Boer War might still be raging in distant South Africa but in England the 'long summer's evening' of the Edwardian era seemed like a continuation of the settled years of the last decades of the 19th century and nothing on the horizon would have indicated the tremendous convulsions which were to dominate the 20th century from 1914 until its end. The Victorian belief in progress seemed vindicated. The obsession with status still remained but Britain was gradually becoming a more open and democratic society. A remarkable example of the new social mobility is the career of David Lloyd George, who had been born on 17th January, 1863, grew up in a small shoemaker's cottage in North Wales and became Chancellor of the Exchequer before he was 50 with neither wealth nor aristocratic birth to support his rise to power.

David Lloyd George, who, indirectly, plays a highly significant part in the story of the life of Joe Lister, was a rare genius but the barriers against succeeding from humble beginnings were being eroded away and it was into this changing world that Joe Lister launched his career. He had, however, one important advantage over many of his fellow citizens at the time. Joe had received the best education that was possible for a boy in his home town of Rotherham and it is perhaps surprising that he does not appear to have immediately capitalised on that when he left school. Had the top boy of Rotherham Grammar School chosen to be articled to a firm of local solicitors, for example, his chances of obtaining such a position would have been very good and he could have had a lucrative, if maybe unexciting, career as a provincial lawyer, or even gone on to become a barrister. Instead he answered an advertisement for a much more lowly position. He writes of it in his 1936 account:

> I left the Grammar School midsummer 1901 and after answering an advertisement for 'Office Boy', asked for under box No., I obtained employment at Joseph Green's, timber merchant, Rotherham, commencing the last Monday in 1901 at 5/- [25p] per week, with the promise of one shilling [5p] per week rise once a year, whether I was worth it or not, Mr. Green saying that this was his starting price, although he admitted my education he thought had fitted me out for something better than he could offer me.

We do not know what was going through the mind of the sixteen year old Joe Lister as he made his way from James' and Ada's house in St Anne's Road through the dimly lit streets of Rotherham dressed in his smart working suit, and clean white shirt with its starched collar, to the firm of Joseph Green for his first day of work on that dark winter's morning of 30th December, 1901. His weekly wage appears miserable but using the average earnings index it would now be equivalent to just over £85 per week. It is difficult to make an exact comparison for the simple reason that life has become so different in the past century and much of what a young man is now able to spend his money on had not even been invented in 1901, but Joe, the future property tycoon, seemed content with this first step on the career ladder and remained in the services of Joseph Green for over twenty years. On that first morning at the premises of the firm, located in George Street, very close to Rotherham Central Station, he would have taken his place in the general office on a high stool and commenced his work at a desk writing invoices and entering items in ledgers. Joe's handwriting was not copperplate but it shows a firm hand and is clearly legible as is shown from the many carbon copies of his letters that have survived. The firm of Joseph Green was in a considerable way of business and was to remain so for some years to come; in the 1920s it had branches in Yorkshire, Lancashire and Lincolnshire as well as one in County Durham and the firm described itself as 'Timber Importer and Saw Miller'. Mr. Joseph Green, who came from Keighley where the business started, was still in charge of the firm when Joe started work but when he died suddenly after being taken ill on a train, his two sons took over the running of the concern; one of them, Wignall Hey Green, is commemorated in the name of one of the earliest roads in Joe's Listerdale Estate – Wignall Avenue.

The promised rise in wages came in August, 1902, as Mr. Green thought Joe worth the increase before the full year was up. During these early years Joe was daily learning what it takes to run a successful business and in October, 1902, an opportunity presented itself. The book-keeper who had come from the Keighley branch of the firm announced his intention of leaving and Joe was approached to take over his duties on a temporary basis in addition to his own work, to which he agreed, but the temporary nature of the post seemed to continue well into the following year and Joe found himself carrying both jobs with no increase in wages. He refrained from making any complaint at this point and successfully produced the firm's balance sheet at the end of the financial year (no mean feat for a seventeen year old) and it was not until Easter that Joseph Green realised that Joe had carried these extra duties without adequate reward and promptly raised his wages to ten shillings (50p) a week saying he was very sorry for the mistake. Showing considerable astuteness and acutely aware that he had done the firm a favour, Joe was not going to let him get away so easily. 'I told him he could not be very sorry otherwise my increase would have dated back to the time I took over [the book-keeper's] duties. After a bit of consideration he smiled and admitted this fact and I went home that weekend with enough money in my pocket – as I thought – to buy the Bank of England.'

Timber was always of great interest to Joe Lister as can be seen by any visitor to the house he built for himself, Castle House, Listerdale, and his knowledge of wood and its uses stems from this period of his working life. He was learning all aspects of the trade from the bottom up and eventually he was not just confined to the office at Joseph Green's, but gained a lot of experience in all the other elements of the trade. It sometimes involved selecting the timber as it stood and the work he undertook would be quite strenuous at times for it included the felling of the timber which, in the days before portable chain-saws, had to be carried out by hand using axes and hand-saws. The machinery that was responsible for the processing of the timber once it had reached the yard was powered by steam-engine, the boiler of which had to be fired constantly to maintain production, and he took his turn at this hard, grimy duty, shovelling coal on to the fire to produce the necessary pressure of steam, becoming for a time like his maternal grandfather, James Shutt the 'engine-tenter'. He was also experienced in operating the actual machinery in the timber-yard which would include some dangerous circular saws. He saw the timber through its whole process from standing tree to its final preparation for leaving the yard on its way to the local goods station of the railway after being sold. It was a steady, if unspectacular, job and he gained promotion, eventually becoming a salesman for the firm where he proved to be very successful, claiming that his sales, in some years, were far in excess of any other salesman they employed. Although nothing in this period of his career gives any clue to his becoming the 'larger than life' character for which he is remembered, except perhaps his success as a salesman, he was steadily laying the foundations of his future success as a businessman.

CHAPTER FIVE:

ROMANCE AND THE OPEN ROAD

In 1906 Joe had saved some money and was able to buy his first motor bike. Over the next few years he bought and exchanged several motor bikes but this is the only one where he informs us of the make, a second-hand NSU which cost him £10. The NSU bikes were made in a small town in southern Germany called Neckarsulm by a company whose primary concern was the manufacture of automatic knitting machines and unsurprisingly it was called the Neckarsulm Strickmaschinen Union (Neckarsulm Knitting Machine Union). When they began to export motor bikes they quickly discovered that it was very difficult to sell a make whose name could not be easily pronounced by non-German speakers so they wisely shortened its name to the initials, NSU. They were a very popular make in the early 1900s when motor-cycling was in its infancy and were fairly lightweight vehicles; Joe gives us no information as to the model he bought but NSU made a very good one with a 500 cc cylinder capacity. The company continued to manufacture motor bikes (and later small cars) in southern Germany until 1957 when the entire motor-cycle division was sold to the Yugoslavians and the former factory in Neckarsulm is now a motor bike museum. Joe's long and absorbing fascination with the internal combustion engine had now begun.

About 18 miles east of Rotherham lies the very small village of Torworth in Nottinghamshire and it straddles the old Great North Road, although little through traffic uses it now with the main A1 bypassing it to the west a few miles away. It would have been busy in the early years of the 20th century, situated as it was on the main thoroughfare from London to Scotland, and in the centre of the village The Huntsman Inn stands right against the main road. Torworth would have been a convenient staging post on the Great North Road between Retford and Bawtry, but the present inn was built around 1900 and it looks very much the same today as it did in the early years of the 20th century when it carried a Royal

The Huntsman Inn, Torworth, c. 1912

Automobile Club enamelled sign informing the traveller that London was 149 miles to the south and the distance to Edinburgh was 245 miles to the north. It was then owned by the Worksop and Retford Brewery and is a substantial, though not very attractive, brick-built two storey building which boasted, in the 1900s, a Club Room, Tap Room and Bar Parlour, together with 'Accommodation for Cyclists' which was painted on the bricks above one of its windows. A large hunting horn hung outside and on the front of the building there was prominently displayed a notice-board on which was inscribed, 'ESTHER SPEAKMAN LICENSED RETAILER OF SPIRITUOUS LIQUOURS AND TOBACCO'.

Esther Speakman had no family connection with Torworth but she came from Leigh in Lancashire, had moved to Nottinghamshire with her husband, Tom, to take over the inn and they had not been landlords very long when, on Easter Saturday, 1912, Joe Lister rolled up on a motor bike with his friend, Bert Douglas, whose machine it happened to be. Joe had bought this particular bike for his friend, Bert, and they were both enjoying the day off work and were out for their first run on it, with Joe thinking he might be able to help if any trouble developed in this second-hand model. The 18 miles had gone very well with no trouble at all and they decided to stop awhile for some refreshment at the Huntsman where, meeting the landlords for the first time, they found that Tom and Esther Speakman were not alone at the inn as their attractive daughter, Mary Evelyne, had come over from Lancashire for the very first time to have a look at the village of Torworth and the Huntsman Inn which was now her parents' home. She had a job in Lancashire as a milliner's assistant but Tom and Esther hoped that she would give that up and come to live in Torworth to help them in the running of their new premises; an attractive barmaid would certainly be good for trade. We do not know whether she had any doubts but she decided to stay on – a decision which turned out to be very important for her. Soon after, her father, Tom, completely disappears from the

Mary Evelyne Lister

scene and there is considerable mystery as to where he went, his place soon being taken by Harold Pierson whom Joe described in his 1936 account as being Mary Evelyne's 'stepfather who lived at the inn with her mother'. Tom Speakman's disappearance from the record would explain why Esther was named on the outside of the building as the licensee of the inn and possibly explains why Mary Evelyne decided with little evident persuasion to stay in Nottinghamshire to help her mother.

Blyth Church

After that first chance visit, Joe was eventually to know every inch of the route from Rotherham to Torworth as it became a regular trip for him on his motor bike, presumably now without any of his friends on the pillion-seat. A romance quickly developed but it was to be two years before Mary Evelyne and he became engaged on Easter Saturday, 1914, an engagement that was not a prolonged one for they were married at the nearby Blyth Parish Church with its imposing 11th century nave and 15th century tower on 16th July, 1914. Joe claimed that he had hoped for a quiet affair, '...but numbers of our friends would not let it be so and came along for the wedding breakfast which was held at the Huntsman Inn.', he wrote in his 1936 account. The wedding was fully reported in the next edition of the *Rotherham Advertiser* on July 18th under the headline, 'Rotherham Man Married at Blyth', a report that clearly underlined Tom Speakman's absence from the scene:

A pretty wedding ceremony took place at Blyth Church on Thursday, the contracting parties being Miss Mary Evelyn(sic) Speakman, only daughter of Mrs. Speakman, of the Huntsman Hotel, Torwarth(sic) and Mr. Joseph C. Lister, eldest son of Mr. and Mrs. James Lister, St. Ann's Road, Rotherham. The wedding party motored to church, the bride looking charming in a grey motoring costume with hat and veil en suite. She was given away by her brother, Mr. Oswald Speakman, Mr Granville Lister, brother of the groom, officiating as best man. Miss Lister and Miss Jessie Lister (sisters of the bridegroom), the former in tan silk poplin and the latter wearing sulphur coloured sponge cloth coatee costume, acted as bridesmaids. Mrs. Speakman, the bride's mother, was gowned in grey with a floral hat; Miss Minnie Barlow was wearing pale blue floral ninon; Mrs. Lister, the bridegroom's mother was in blue and Mrs. Toothill in white. Miss Briggs (Ranskill) and Miss Ida Truss (Doncaster) were each in pretty grey costumes. A reception was held at the bride's home, the "Huntsman", Torwarth, at which upwards of thirty guests were entertained. The happy pair later left by motor en route for Bridlington, where the honeymoon is being spent.

As was the general custom in 1914, the presents received by the couple were all listed in the newspaper and many were very handsome ones. Mary Evelyne had bought Joe a dressing case and Joe had bought his wife a diamond ring. Among the guests was Bert Douglas, without whom the wedding may never have taken place but for that first visit of Joe's to Torworth on Bert's motor bike where he met his future bride. Minnie Barlow, no doubt looking very beautiful in her 'pale blue floral ninon', a lightweight silk fabric, later became Joe's sister-in-law when she married Granville Lister. The list of presents was very full with Harold Pierson's gift listed right behind that of the bridegroom's father:

> ...bride's mother, household linen, rug, etc.; bridegroom's mother, furniture and silver tea and coffee service; bridegroom's father, cheque and sideboard; Mr. Pierson, cheque; Miss Barlow and Mr. G. Lister, dinner service; Miss Lister, tea set and ormolu clock; Miss J. Lister, toilet set; Mr. and Mrs. R. Toothill, Grecian standard lamp; Miss P. Bradley (Manchester), silver café terre(sic); Mr. Gilbert Lister, brass letter rack; Master Donald Lister, photo frame; Mr. Harris Foster, cheque; Mr. and Mrs. Crippen (Manchester), salad bowl and servers; Miss E. M. Crippen (Manchester), cutlery; Miss S. Crippen (Manchester), tablecloth; Mr. T. Whitehead, silver tablespoons; Mr. Lowe and Mr. D. O. Speakman, set of bronzes and brass plant stand; Mr Harrie Foster, Mr Reg. Allan and friends, black skin rugs; Mr. and Mrs. Frank Oxley, antique bronze curb and irons; Mr. and Mrs. Frank Watson, silver teapot; Mr. Bert Douglas, Mr. Matt Thom, and Mr. Jack Wallace, dining table; Mr. Chas. Spearing, kitchen utensils; Mr. Hubert Speakman, vases.

At the time of his wedding Joe had graduated to four-wheeled transport and they set off on their honeymoon to Bridlington, a place that was to become almost as important as Rotherham in Joe's story, in one of Joe's early cars, a light 'tandem' two-seater Sabella, before coming back to Torworth to begin their married life together at the Huntsman Inn.

**Joe in his honeymoon car, a 1914 Sabella.
The passenger sat in front of the driver**

Joe was still working at Joseph Green's and he would now have to commute the 18 miles morning and evening from Torworth to Rotherham and back to continue with his job, (although as he was now a salesman for the firm he would undoubtedly sometimes start his commercial travelling without the need for going to the timber yard at Rotherham) a situation which would have been impossible only a few years before but the introduction of cars and motor bikes on English roads was beginning to open up many new horizons and possibilities as longer distance commuting gradually became viable.

Joe and Mary Evelyne would have been so pre-occupied with their wedding arrangements that they would not have recognised the significance of an event which had taken place just over two weeks before the moment when they were standing together in front of the altar to be joined in holy matrimony in Blyth Church. In a city called Sarajevo, which few in Rotherham would even have heard of at the time, the heir to the Austro-Hungarian throne, Archduke Francis Ferdinand, was assassinated by a fanatical Bosnian nationalist, Gavrilo Princip. The fragile stability of Western Europe was beginning to shake to its foundations, but England was in the middle of a gorgeous summer and the gathering clouds were not disturbing the nation's enjoyment, even though, after that fatal pistol shot in the Bosnian capital, the drift to war was accelerating as threats, counter-threats and mobilisations increased across the continent of Europe. For most people in England war was unthinkable at the time. The international settlement which had been reached after the Napoleonic conflagrations a century earlier had largely endured, buttressed by the unrivalled power of the British Empire and there was an unspoken belief that nothing could ever come along to challenge that British supremacy. Few had the foresight to realise the significance of the emergence of a German Empire which followed the defeat of France in the Franco-Prussian War of 1870-71, a war in which Britain had not been involved. After all, had not England for a very long time been as Shakespeare had described in *Richard II*: 'a fortress built by nature for herself against infection and the hand of war'? That glorious carefree summer of 1914 came to an abrupt end on August 4th, not many days after Joe and his bride had returned from their honeymoon, when Britain found itself at war, this time in Europe. It was a war that was to change society for ever and, indirectly, it was to change the fortunes of the Lister family.

CHAPTER SIX:

THE LISTERS IN WARTIME

Very soon after the start of the war Joe volunteered to enlist but in September, 1914, he was taken ill with kidney stones, a problem that arose, according to his doctor, from spending so much time on his motor bike and being subject to the chilling effect of the wind as motoring clothing in those early days offered little protection. If true, no doubt this resulted from his very frequent visits to Torworth to win the hand of Mary Evelyne. The army medical board rejected him: he was found to be only of grade 3 fitness, later downgraded to 4 in his case, and he never served in the armed forces. His brothers also volunteered with more success and James Granville, who had served in the 'Territorials' prior to the 1914, later claimed that he was the first man to enlist in the West Riding Horse Artillery and one of the original members of the 'Maltby War Pals'; the creation of 'Pals Battalions' was a device for keeping together men who had been recruited from localities when they served at the front and was very successful at keeping up morale in the most horrible circumstances of trench warfare. All of the Lister brothers survived the war; their names never needed to be inscribed on the vast number of war memorials that now remind us of the carnage of that terrible conflict.

Most thought, in the autumn of 1914, that the men 'would be home by Christmas' and the war would be little more than something of a skirmish which the British, with their skill at handling the small wars of Empire, would be able to deal with very quickly. Only a very few could see that August, 1914, was a time of great foreboding with 'the lights going out all over Europe' and that the world was in for a prolonged conflict. At the end of that conflict the casualty toll for Britain and its Empire was 2.7 million, of which over 900,000 were fatal. The Lister family were rare in that they were not personally affected by tragedy.

Historians have debated long and hard over the causes of the First World War but it soon became apparent that the course of the war was not going all that well for the Allies in the early stages. Losses at the front were enormous and by December, 1916, the British Government led by Herbert Henry Asquith was in serious trouble and he found himself no longer able to command the confidence of the House of Commons. The political crisis was resolved by the formation of a coalition government led by David Lloyd George, who had previously been Minister of Munitions and later Secretary of State for War and whose political rise had been remarkable. First elected to Parliament for Caernavon Boroughs in North Wales in 1890, David Lloyd George had entered the Cabinet in 1905 as President of the Board of Trade immediately on the formation of the Liberal Government under Sir Henry Campbell-Bannerman. In 1908 he had become Chancellor of the Exchequer, a post he still occupied at the start of the war in 1914. Unlike Winston Churchill in 1945, he won a convincing victory after the war at the general election in 1918, when women were allowed to vote for the first time, provided they were over 30. Joe Lister and Lloyd George never met but it was the measures for national reconstruction that the 'Welsh Wizard' was to take in 1919 that were to be the beginning

of the transformation in the life and fortunes of Joe
Lister and his family (see Appendix, p 193).

The war at the front was a slaughterhouse for the
soldiers who were taking part in it but British civilians
at home were not in great danger, unlike the 1939-45
war. Aerial warfare was in its infancy. There was some
bombardment of coastal towns from enemy warships in
the English Channel and the North Sea and there was
also the Zeppelin. This was an airship developed by
Ferdinand, Graf Von Zeppelin, who was a German
military officer with a great interest in balloon flight.
He had developed it commercially before the war and
the German High Command used it to mount air-raids
over Britain. The Zeppelin was a large and slow moving
dirigible which proved a sitting target to anti-aircraft
fire and it was also kept aloft by the highly flammable
hydrogen gas. Nevertheless, the Germans attempted a
raid on Sheffield and on Retford, 5 miles south of
Torworth, and Joe records how he and his family
watched both of these Zeppelin raids from the bedroom
windows at Torworth. It was the nearest they came to
the realities of war during that period.

The Huntsman Inn's contribution to the war effort took
the form of refusing to pass on any increase in the price
of drinks to the soldiers who were stationed nearby at
Barnby Moor, the next village south of Torworth. Soon
after that an aerodrome was built at Babworth, a village
on the way to Retford, to accommodate the growing
numbers serving in the Royal Flying Corps, the
forerunner of the Royal Air Force. Many of these troops
used the Huntsman where they were able to buy drinks
sold to them at a price that was actually lower than

the Brewery Company charged the inn. However, Esther Speakman did not have to stand the loss as, according to Joe's own account of those days, the Brewery Company made it good on each settlement day.

Harold Pierson may have been referred to by Joe as his wife's stepfather and he certainly took the place of Tom Speakman at the Huntsman Inn but there was no divorce and therefore no marriage between Esther and Harold following Tom's departure from their lives. Joe's 1936 account actually says Harold Pierson was 'afterwards my wife's stepfather, who lived at the Inn with her mother' and this might imply that a marriage took place much later but there is no memory of that event in the family. Harold was experienced in the manufacture of torpedoes, having worked overseas for some years until 1912 as an employee of Whitehead's, the torpedo manufacturers, (Robert Whitehead began developing self-propelled torpedoes in 1864) in the Adriatic port of Fiume; this port is now called Rijeka and is the principal commercial port of Croatia but in the early 20th century it was part of the Austro-Hungarian Empire. It was not long before he offered his services to the British Government and left Torworth for Greenock on the River Clyde where he was once more involved in the production of torpedoes.

Without the support of Harold, Esther Speakman found it very hard to maintain the Huntsman. She carried on for a few months but then felt that she would have to surrender the licence as the work was too much for her. Inn-keeping is a very demanding trade, involving long hours with still much work to be done after closing time. Undoubtedly she had help and would at least need a cellar-man to deal with the heavy beer barrels, even if she could manage the bar-work herself with the help of Mary Evelyne, but we can imagine the extra work involved as hordes of servicemen descended on the inn at opening time and she might have needed help to deal with the odd one or two who drank more than was good for them. It all became more than she could manage and she asked the Worksop and Retford Brewery Company to find a replacement. Despite advertising, no-one came forward and Joe then had a bright idea. He volunteered his wife. He spoke to the secretary of the company, a Mr Blundell, and informed him that if he spoke nicely to Mary Evelyne she would be prepared to undertake the duties involved in running the inn. Joe recognised that it was not the sort of job that his wife really liked but he was obviously very persuasive for they took over the licence on Easter Saturday, 1915. Joe could now add 'publican' to his record of employment.

The war curtailed imports into Britain and the timber trade did not escape these restrictions which had their effects on Joe's employers, Joseph Green, forcing them to concentrate on the use of home grown timber. One unintended result of this was that it gave Joe far more experience of the timber trade from beginning to end. Now, he was not only involved in the processes that were carried out at the saw mills, but gained considerable experience, as he put it, by being 'mixed up with a lot of the felling, leading and converting of this class of timber [home grown].' Throughout his career Joe was known for his understanding of various woods and their properties and undoubtedly his knowledge was enhanced by his experience during these war years.

In the middle of all the reports of the dreadful loss of life at the front in France there occurred an important cause for celebration in Joe's life during these war years - the start of his own family. Mary Evelyne's and Joe's first child, Marjorie Greenhough Lister, was born on May 14th, 1917, at the Huntsman Inn followed by a son, Clifford James Lister, who was born almost two years later on May 20th, 1919. Marjorie was given her second name of Greenhough after the maiden name of her grandmother, Esther Speakman.

CHAPTER SEVEN:

THE WOODEN HUT

When war ended on November 11th, 1918, life began to adjust slowly to peacetime routines. The General Election of 1918, called immediately after the armistice, returned the Lloyd George Coalition with a substantial majority, although it was heavily dependent on the support of the Conservatives who were, in fact, the largest party after the election; they were eventually to topple David Lloyd George in October, 1922, forming their own government under, at first, Andrew Bonar Law and, later, Stanley Baldwin. Life at the Huntsman Inn in Torworth resumed its steady pace and Joe continued with his work selling timber for Joseph Green. He had over the years become a very successful salesman for the firm and his income was by now much improved from the pittance on which he started. As a salesman he was entitled to bonuses depending on his success and he records that from time to time he received £500 in bonus which would have been a considerable sum for a young man to receive in 1918, and he was now becoming reasonably prosperous as a result of his hard work and loyalty to his employers, with whom he had now worked for nearly twenty years. His position in life, if unspectacular, seemed assured and, as long as timber was required, he could look forward to a very solid and comfortable future. As the war ended, there was nothing in his record up to that point that would indicate the entrepreneurial turn his life was later to take. However, matters were even then being discussed at the highest levels of government which would prove to be the springboard to a most significant development in his career (see Appendix, pp 191-193).

The Lister family situation had changed very much since 1915 when they took over the public house and Mary Evelyne in her turn must have found it extremely difficult to cope with all the work involved in looking after two small children as well as the running of the Huntsman Inn. That was at a time when no husband was expected to provide much practical assistance in the home and life was very much divided between 'man's work' and 'woman's work', although that did not stop Mary Evelyne from running the inn. Joe's daughter, Marjorie, remembers that throughout her childhood her father was always so pre-occupied with work and business that he spent very little time with his children. He later referred to this himself by writing in his account dated 1936 that 'if my children compare me to the fathers of other children they know, I dare say from the actual fatherly interest I take in them, I do not show to advantage'. He went on to plead that business worries (which were to come later) had prevented his spending enough time with them. He was probably doing himself something of an injustice as the early 20th century was still a time when fathers were to be respected and even feared. Indeed, King George V is reputed to have declared that he had been frightened of his father and was going to make sure his own children were frightened of him. Joe was not all that out of the ordinary in this respect and later he proved to be not unmindful of the plight of women who were left at home all day. 'Having been mixed up with rent collecting for a great many years of my life, I have realised how trying the life of a woman can be who has to stay in the house practically all day with no-one to speak to', he wrote in 1936.

Whatever Joe felt, Mary Evelyne eventually persuaded him that running the Huntsman Inn was too much for her and Joe informed the brewery company that they wished to leave. Joe was reluctant, which is not surprising as they had no other home at the time but Mary Evelyne convinced him that the inn was not paying its way, even though she had managed to save a few hundred pounds while she had been running the establishment. Whatever arguments they had between them over the issue, they were ready to leave in 1921 and, as Joe records, they received in valuation three times the amount they had paid to the brewery when they went into the business six years previously – a very useful nest-egg.

When they were ready to leave the Huntsman, Joe Lister, the future entrepreneur, property developer and landlord to 800 tenants, was 35 years old and had sold a lot of timber but had never built or owned a house. By his own account his ambitions in 1921 in the direction of property ownership seemed to be limited. 'At the time we decided to leave the inn I was on the look-out for a small piece of land upon which to erect a single residence and run a few fowls, pigs, etc., as I had been doing at Torworth', he wrote later. With his extensive knowledge of working in wood it is no surprise to discover that he was planning a timber house and one that he would build himself. It would have to be large enough to accommodate his family and provide the necessary amenities and comforts suitable for life in the 1920s. It is also no surprise that he was thinking of somewhere in the Rotherham area close to where he was born and where he worked. But how could this small piece of land to be found and how much would it all cost? The money Mary Evelyne had saved while running the Huntsman, and the money received from the valuation on vacating the inn together with the money saved from Joe's generous bonuses from Joseph Green provided a basis from which to work. It could all be just possible.

The village of Wickersley is about 4 miles to the east of Rotherham along the Bawtry Road, the present A631. It is an ancient village and is mentioned in the Domesday Book where it is listed, along with many Yorkshire manors, as being completely waste and valueless. Times have changed and it is now a busy suburb for, as a result of local government re-organisation, it has in recent years been absorbed into the Metropolitan Borough of Rotherham. In 1912 a trolleybus or 'trackless' service began operating from Rotherham running through the village to Maltby, a few miles further on the road towards Bawtry, but Wickersley in the 1920s remained in a distinctly rural situation with considerable tracts of farmland between the village and the eastern edges of the town of Rotherham. The main thoroughfare was made into a turnpike road in 1760 and was an important route for goods from Sheffield to the river port at Bawtry on the River Idle, from where they could connect to the River Trent and eventually the Humber and the seaport of Kingston-upon-Hull. At the top of the hill coming out of Rotherham there had once been a toll gate, the memory of which is preserved in the name of a nearby road, Toll Bar Road. Near to the site of the old toll house there now stands the Brecks Hotel, a 1930s building erected on the land once occupied by Brecks Farm and a little further along the road are the remains of some old stone-quarries. The stone industry had once been a very important in the area of the village, employing a considerable number of people; the Directory of 1871 lists no fewer than 28 quarry owners in the parish. Underlying the whole geology of the area is a stone of very high quality called 'Wickersley Rock' which had long been used in building but was also discovered to make very good fine-grained grindstones and so great was the demand for stone of this quality from the cutlery industry in Sheffield that at one time 5,000 grindstones a year were transported from Wickersley to Sheffield. Stone had been quarried in the Brecks for many years but by 1921 the quarries were falling into disuse as the Sheffield cutlers were turning towards emery wheels for grinding their knives to a fine edge, and trees were rapidly growing over the old workings on the site of the old quarry. The area still retains its name of 'The Brecks' which may well refer to the quarrying activity that was carried out there for many years and could be derived from a Germanic root meaning 'to break'.

Joe Lister would have had little cause to visit The Brecks in the course of his work in the timber trade, and by 1921 the old quarries and adjoining wood, known as Daffy Woods, had been bought by a Mr Archibald Blenkinsop who was not interested in the stone but in the trees. He had felled them for use as pit props for the underground workings at the nearby Silverwood Colliery. He needed a crane to load the logs onto the transport used to take them to the colliery and had purchased a second-hand one from Joseph Green. It was very early in 1921 and the weather was cold but Joe and his friend, Mr Toothill, decided to visit the old quarries at the Brecks to see how Mr Blenkinsop was managing with the firm's old crane. They both stood on a rough hill-top and surveyed the scene when Toothill suddenly turned to Joe and said, 'How is this piece of land for what you want?'

On that wintry morning in 1921 it seemed a bleak and isolated spot and demanded a great deal of imagination to see it as a suitable place to build a house, let alone to be described as 'a perfect little arcadia' as it was only a few years later in the *Country Illustrated*. The terrain was rough with much of it scarred with the remains of years of stone workings but it was close to some pleasant woodland, streams and valleys and the idea intrigued Joe. Would the owner, Blenkinsop, sell it for a price that Joe could afford to pay? He decided to approach him with the idea and so he telephoned him, arranging to meet on the site the following Saturday afternoon. Blenkinsop was a shrewd operator who could drive a hard bargain and what followed was a deal which most definitely turned in a handsome profit for him. Having sold the trees, the land would offer little more return for him if he kept it, but the area of the old quarries and wood amounted to just over 44 acres and some of it was still yielding stone which he was selling for providing the foundations for road-making. At first Blenkinsop was only prepared to sell a small part of it as he wished to keep selling the stone. Joe was having none of this and countered with the observation that the part Blenkinsop wished to keep would spoil the shape of the portion he was prepared to sell to Joe so consequently no deal could be closed on that basis. Eventually the whole of the 44 acres became Joe's for £750 and he now had his foot on the first rung of the property ladder – even though it was far more than the 'small piece of land' he had envisaged. Joe knew that his first land transaction was a good deal for Blenkinsop as he was later to observe when looking back on that time: 'I was given to understand that he originally paid somewhere about £450 for it, which he had received back for the timber and stone sold off it, so I think he made a profit'. Blenkinsop thought Joe's intention to build a house on such an isolated spot was a touch eccentric and forecast that Mary Evelyne would raise considerable objections to it, but Joe knew that she was desperate to leave the Huntsman Inn and when he told her what he was intending she took the view that she would put up with the situation rather than continue selling beer in Torworth.

Joe had used the money he had received in bonuses and the money his wife had saved, together with the amount received on valuation when they relinquished the licence of the inn, to purchase the site and now build his home. There was certainly more than enough land to build a house and run the livestock he intended and there is no clue that there was anything more in his mind at this point. Once the sale was agreed he lost no time and as a man well versed in the timber trade it is no surprise that he immediately began to design and build a sectional hut of wooden framing with asbestos sheeting on the outside, the overall dimensions being 28 feet by 16 feet, which was to stand on short brick stilts. As he was an employee of Joseph Green he would have been able to do all this on very advantageous terms. His family would now see little of him for some time because, after spending his working day with the firm, he stayed there in the evenings after work and also went back at weekends to construct the various sections of his hut and he tells us that it all took 'the following week or two'. The house he was designing was a bungalow, a style of building that had become more popular throughout the 19th century and, after being originally introduced into Britain as a sort of holiday retreat or weekend home for those who could afford one, was gradually assuming its own place as an alternative design for permanent residences alongside the more conventional two-storey house. What official permission he needed for the construction of such a building on the land he had bought is not recorded but it is a matter of fact that in the 1920s rural district councils were rather lax in the conditions they enforced for the building of asbestos bungalows. Joe never intended the hut as anything more than a temporary home, until he could afford a brick built residence, obviously thinking that any more permanent dwelling would be built virtually on the same site, for he had plans to convert the wood and asbestos hut into a playroom for Marjorie and Clifford, with half of it serving as a garage as well.

Records show that Joe did not complete the purchase of the land until 21st March, 1921. Easter was early in that year and they had to vacate the inn by then, but it is obvious that Joe must have been working very hard on constructing the sections of his hut long before he entered into complete possession of the land, for it was all ready to be assembled immediately he could obtain access to the site. Joe managed to borrow Joseph Green's lorry to transport it and he was busy putting it all together four days later on Good Friday, March 25th, with the help of a man he had brought over from

Torworth, when to his horror he discovered that the bolts for the roof-ridge were missing, having been lost in transit. All the ironmongers were closed on Good Friday and it was impossible to find replacement bolts in time so there was little he could do that day but to cover the roof as much as possible with felt, leaving the ridge piece unbolted, and then hope for a fine night. It turned out to be a forlorn hope. The furniture van was expected soon and it duly arrived late in the afternoon, but as they began to unload the contents the heavens opened and rain poured in through the ridge. Doubtless intent on putting the finishing touches to the construction and making it secure, the two men had failed to notice until it was far too late that water was pouring onto one of the beds and it had become so completely soaked that Joe felt he was left with no alternative at that stage but to turn the bed over and hope that the water drained out in time. He had yet to face Mary Evelyne.

The next day was an extremely eventful one for Joe. It was Easter Saturday, March 26th, and he had to work at Joseph Green's. It was also the day that they were to vacate the Huntsman Inn. Early in the morning he drove himself, Mary Evelyne, Marjorie and Clifford over to the hut and left them there, apparently not telling his wife about the soaking of the previous night, and went off to work, probably to be out of the way. He came back at noon to find a tearful and no doubt furious Mary Evelyne wanting to know why the bed in which they had slept on Thursday night at the inn was wet through on Saturday morning. It was also badly stained as Joe had casually tossed a double-barrelled shot-gun on the bed as he left on Good Friday and it had rusted with the rain, leaving its imprint behind. He had a real problem on his hands explaining what had happened with his wife declaring that they could not possibly stay there as they would all definitely die of pneumonia. It was a bad start and it took all of Joe's powers of persuasion to get her to remain in the hut but they lit a big fire to dry out the bed and everything else that had become damp and they stayed. The bolts were eventually found and the hut was finally made waterproof.

Today, no trace of that wooden hut remains. The area where it stood, at the top of Hollins Hill Lane but still quite secluded even now, is occupied by several modern detached bungalows and the Bawtry Road, which has over the years become an extremely busy dual carriageway, is approximately 100 yards away. Marjorie, who would have been nearly six years old when she moved there from Torworth with her parents, remembers the hut very well as having a kitchen with a stove, a big living room with a large dining table, three bedrooms and a verandah. It was heated by coal fires and had an inside toilet which would have been something of a rarity in a simply built dwelling of 1921. Marjorie also remembers that at the time the Lister family moved in there were no other houses in the vicinity.

What ambitions Joe fostered at this time it is impossible to tell but he now owned a considerable amount of land and was settled near his home town. It was the simple beginning of his future property empire even though, in 1921, he lacked the resources to exploit his property and had his family to look after. He would be dependent on his job at Joseph Green's for some time to come but he proved to be a man who could seize an opportunity when it was presented to him and, with a Government desperate to solve a crisis in housing, such an opportunity was just round the corner.

PART TWO: OPPORTUNITIES

CHAPTER EIGHT:

'IT ONLY STARTED BECAUSE I HAD A WIFE'

There is a tide in the affairs of men
Which taken at the flood leads on to fortune
William Shakespeare, *Julius Caesar*, Act IV, Scene iii

The exact point when Joe Lister decided to venture out into deeper waters and create a housing estate on the outskirts of Rotherham is impossible to ascertain but it must have come very close on the heels of his move from Torworth. His career up to that point had been an extremely steady one, working for the same employer for twenty years and rising slowly through the firm until he was receiving a very comfortable income. During the whole of those twenty years he had shown little inclination for taking risks but now, whether he fully realised it at the time or not, he was about to embark on the biggest venture of his life, one whose effect would be to add an extra name to the maps of South Yorkshire. 'Listerdale' was a name invented by Joe and his first recorded use of it occurs less than a year after he had built his wooden hut and it is contained in a letter written by Joe to Sir Alfred Mond MP, dated March 6th, 1922. At some point soon after he moved from Torworth Joe had acquired a hand embossing device in order to make his personal notepaper look more professional and the paper on which this particular letter is written is duly embossed with his new address, 'J. C. LISTER. LISTERDALE. Nr. ROTHERHAM'. Mond had succeeded Addison as Minister of Health in April, 1921,

66

and Joe was seeking an extension of the subsidy that was then paid to private builders (see Appendix, p 193). It was the first of his several attempts to involve the Government in his housing scheme.

Building houses has always been a risky business for it involves a huge outlay before there is any hope of a return. Bankruptcy is common in the industry and builders constantly experience cash flow problems. Joe, although brought up surrounded by the building trade, was not a professional builder at this point in his life. He knew a great deal about timber following his twenty years working in that trade, but his knowledge of all the other aspects involved in the building of houses was not as yet at first-hand. He may well have financed the construction of his wooden residence from his own resources and those of Mary Evelyne's but he needed to raise considerably more finance even to contemplate the building of an estate of houses. Where he obtained his earliest loans is not clear but it was not very long before he needed to raise more money and a four page letter to the Halifax Permanent Building Society, written in a style which was to become very characteristic of him, contains many clues to his thinking at this time but it is rather confusingly dated. The first three pages are dated 'Jan 8/22' but the fourth page carries the date of January 8th, 1923. It is possible that Joe was making a very common mistake, forgetting, as many people still do particularly when writing cheques, that by January he was in a new year, for the later date makes more sense. The reply from the Building Society would also support the later date for it is itself dated 9th January, 1923. Joe's letter makes very clear that he was by then following the example of his grandfather, 'Old Joe', and was engaged in building a whole estate of houses which he intended to sell to owner-occupiers, as the letter on his embossed Listerdale notepaper is headed 'With reference to the above estate'. It is also very clear from the text that he had included some of 'Old Joe's' 1889 leaflets to support his case. He presents a rather unusual proposition and asks the Halifax for an advance of £5,000 'against the whole estate', most of which was as yet unbuilt, and suggests that he would be able to pay it back within ten years 'not to be a definite sum each week, but in any manner so long as before the specified date'. The letter seeks to assure the Building Society that his prospective estate would be a safe investment for their money and it continues by making clear that he still expected to carry on his 'day job' working at Joseph Green's whilst engaged on the building of houses:

> I have run this job as a one man show and am anxious to see it through as such and as my nest eggs are in this basket you may rest assured I am looking after the handle.
>
> My employment is the timber trade from which and other sources...is £800 per year income so that I am not working to margins and my chief reason for asking for a lump [sum] is so that I can erect 10 or 12 [houses] at a time without hopping round the corner every time I want some money.
>
> I asked the Government to lend me £20,000, but their reply was that under section 67 of the Working Classes Housing Act of 1890 there was nothing doing as my clients weren't workers (Ye Gods! And some of the poor devils kick off at 8.0 a.m. and carry on till 9.0 p.m. but forget to come home with black faces and trousers seats missing, hence the above results).
>
> This letter doesn't sound much like business in places, but accept my apologies please as I am cursed or blessed with hoary ancestors who had bats in the belfry as the enclosed leaflets will testify (which kindly return as their value as ancient curious (sic) is equal to the relics ex the Tombs at Luxor) so you will understand that I am not responsible for my action when housing is under discussion.

Wignall Green, Joe's employer

The £800 per annum which Joe mentions as his income in 1923 would have put him in the 'well-to-do' class at a time when most men would have counted themselves lucky to be able to take home £2 per week. It is abundantly clear from this correspondence that Joe had quickly moved on from his desire to 'erect a single residence and run a few fowls, pigs etc.' for by the date of this letter (taking the 1923 date) he had completed 18 houses 'all built during last 15 months'. These first houses he sold and drew a ground rent of £7.00 per annum per house in addition to £26 per annum rent from 'one small one' which he had let, the first recorded instance of his building a house for renting. This was a low-density development of no more than four houses per acre and his purchasers would have been salaried and professional. In his letter, he hopes that his solicitors, Oxley and Coward of Rotherham, 'will perhaps confirm what I say' but was writing to the Building Society 'direct in this instance so that I know my case will be stated as I wish' and includes an offer to come over and see them. 'All the building is done by direct labour and as I am Architect, Clerk of Works, Cashier, Secretary, Buyer, etc., whatever profit out of the job belongs', is how he concludes the letter to the Halifax and asks for an early reply. The Building Society certainly complied with his last request and was interested enough to reply by return with a letter signed by Enoch Hill, the Secretary of the Society at the time. They returned his leaflets but, perhaps not surprisingly, they did not grant this particular application on Joe's terms. It is very obvious from the tone of their reply that they would sooner see the houses built first, for he was as yet an untried property developer and the directors of the Halifax were not prepared to advance all the money in a single sum in order for him to build the estate. Neither were they ready to risk such a large amount on the terms of Joe's unusual repayment proposition but, interestingly, they did not turn him down completely and informed Joe that they were ready to consider 'applications on separate blocks as they are erected' as well as assuring him that the mortgages would be 'upon the usual terms and conditions and certainly nothing less than 6% would be acceptable at present for interest charges'.

Joe's solicitors, Oxley and Coward, whom he mentioned in the letter, may well have confirmed all that Joe had written to the Halifax Permanent Benefit Building Society, as it was known at the time, and Joe was at the beginning of a long relationship with this particular firm of Rotherham solicitors but it was not to be all sweetness and light. As early as April, 1925, he was complaining vigorously of their treatment of him after there had obviously been something of a quarrel. In a long letter dated April 4th and addressed to 'Dear Pickles' he was grumbling about what he saw as their lack of attention to his business. It is also clear that he was very dependent on his bank for the necessary capital to commence the building of each house:

From the very commencement of our business I have worked to the limit of my capital and the assistance you have given in the speeding up of the cash from the Bldg. Society has been anything but satisfactory, as on several occasions I have made enquiries and whereas the blame in delay has been put on the Bldg. Society it has been caused in your office or at Doncaster and consequently instead of receiving my cash in a reasonable time to pay the Bank I do nothing but manufacture excuses as to why it has not been paid in, which excuses do not improve my credit. You stated the delay was caused by the haphazard way I gave you instructions, which if put into writing would facilitate matters (in this last instance this was done, but the result is just the same) so I conclude my business does not appeal to you, otherwise it would have a better share of attention.

In our business when we cannot give the customer the attention he is entitled to we are not surprised if he goes elsewhere and in my case and yourselves I am aware you have far bigger fish in your pond than I shall be, being only Trout size, but a Trout among a shoal of Minnows looks a damn big fish and I know plenty of streams with nowt (sic) but Minnows in.

Advantage is taken of the fact that I haven't the time to come and pester your guts out and I only call when things are at the far end, after, to my mind, giving you ample time to deal with the matter in hand.

This last case is a typical one in point – you are so interested in my affairs that you don't know whether you have some of my deeds or not and to hide this defect in your knowledge you accuse me of not giving a square deal. A square deal my lad is one with four corners on it and you have never had any other variety from me although if it comes to passing money deals as square ones I'd like to bet a quid or two that a cock-eyed chap at Listerdale could pull off a lot more than the next man, anyhow more attention to my affairs from your side is and has been required and if you are not particularly interested in them say so and I know what to do.

There is no record of any reply to this onslaught which no doubt established from an early date how Joe wished his business to be conducted. Oxley and Coward continued to act for him, which was no doubt a wise decision on their part as Joe was to provide them with an enormous amount of business as his estate developed over the years. The relationship was often a difficult one, but Arthur Pickles, to whom the above diatribe was addressed, eventually became a lifelong friend and Oxley and Coward were prepared, at times, to advance Joe some of the capital he needed in the form of bridging loans to cover the period between the agreed sale of houses and the actual receipt of money from the purchasers. This was often a complex arrangement and in the 1930 account of his affairs Joe stated that although he had 'neither the desire nor intention to impute anything dishonourable to Oxley and Coward', he felt that there was room for improvement in their methods of book-keeping, complaining that they never sent him an official statement of account.

Joe was also operating as his own estate agent and selling his properties as they were completed. In a letter to one prospective purchaser, dated May 18th, 1926, he explains that his 'scheme at Listerdale is out of the ordinary as it comprises 100 acres of recreation ground' which he had bought and that in order for him to keep some control over the class of purchaser he had made the land leasehold for 200 years with each bungalow or house standing in a plot of '800 to 1000 square yards according to the situation'. In the same letter he invites an inspection of his development, informing the likely purchaser that 'the Maltby to Rotherham buses pass the Estate', and reveals the considerable pressures under which he must have been working for 'being in business in the Timber Trade rather handicaps me for time to give to the building side'.

He would have been fully aware of the Government's measures to solve the housing crisis by subsidy and was determined to profit from it, for these early houses in Listerdale were certainly built under the Addison scheme (see Appendix, p 193) and it is also abundantly clear from the timing of events that he was forced to work extremely fast to qualify for the subsidy before it ran out. It amounted to £240 or £260 per house, depending upon size, which would have taken care of a large proportion of the actual building costs at the time. The scheme was in full swing when the Lloyd George Government surprised everyone by suddenly announcing in April, 1921, that, because of the drain on the public finances at a time of economic slump, it would be abruptly withdrawing the subsidies on July 1st, 1921, which was less than three months after Joe had built his first property, the wooden hut. It did, however, make one very important concession which Joe was able to exploit to advantage. Local authorities were to lose their subsidies on the building of council houses at the end of June but special dispensation was given to the building of any private houses provided they were commenced by August 31st, 1921, and Joe quickly realised that if he had at least laid the foundations by that date he would qualify for the generous grant. He could not afford to waste any time and he needed to recruit enough labour to carry out the necessary work before the closure date. 'I immediately drew plans for eight or nine types of house and bungalow and put the foundations in for 40 houses, for which I had only ten days time in which to do it. The older part of Listerdale are the bungalows built under this scheme,' he wrote in 1936 – that means he had to lay foundations for four houses each day and they all had to be dug and laid by hand.

What other triggers might there have been to cause Joe to start this major project? His daughter, Marjorie, recalls that near the end of his life he had told her that he thought it 'would never have started if I hadn't had a wife'. A clue to what he might have meant by that remark comes from his 1936 account. Mary Evelyne soon began to complain that 'the situation of the hut was too lonely' and persuaded Joe to build another house for them nearer the main road. Further land would need to be purchased in order to do this as the suitable building land in the old quarries did not extend far enough. The adjoining field of about six acres was owned by Mr W. H. Roddis and Joe bought it from him for the sum of £450. It was excellent building land with room for up to two dozen houses at a density of four to the acre. Today, Marcliff Crescent with its pleasant bungalows set in an abundance of trees occupies the site and it is hard to imagine it as an empty field. The crescent and its close derive their names from a combination of those of his two children, Marjorie and Clifford. An adjoining road he was to call Wignall Avenue as a tribute to his employer, Wignall Hey Green, who had succeeded his father as the proprietor of Joseph Green's. He had every reason for showing this gratitude as Wignall Green had shown great consideration to the young Joe Lister, being prepared to stand as guarantor for loans necessary to finance his enterprise, eventually lending him money himself and allowing him virtually unlimited credit for the timber required for the building operations. At one point Joe owed him a total of £16,000, none of which was secured, a substantial sum in the 1930s. Without such friends as these Joe could only have realised a fraction of his achievement. Joe commented in 1936, long after he had left his employment, that 'without the help of my late employer, Mr Wignall Hey Green, Listerdale as it now stands would have been absolutely impossible'.

Wignall Avenue in the 1920s

Joe's acquisition of land was only just starting and he very quickly bought a neighbouring farm of 170 acres in the

Dalton Denes area for which he paid the substantial sum of £3,000. He was in obvious need of raising finance from various sources for all these acquisitions, and that might have been the reason for his letter to the Halifax in January, 1923. In that same letter he refers to the farm he had purchased which was let to a tenant farmer, a Mr Somerset, and Joe was receiving £130 a year in rent. He now commenced the building of a second home for himself and his family which still stands, although much altered, and is now 14 Marcliff Crescent. Alas for Joe, he and Mary Evelyne could not agree on what now appears to be a very minor point, the use of one of the rooms in the new house. The disagreement proved impossible to resolve and there was therefore no alternative but to put this new house up for sale before they had lived in it and begin again. He had no trouble selling it, having advertised the house in the paper of August Bank Holiday Saturday and by Sunday morning it had been sold to a Mr Pontis. With the proceeds of this sale Joe bought a further adjoining field of approximately 3 acres which abutted the main road and he then commenced the building of a bungalow with a large garden very close to Bawtry Road, the residence which in a few years evolved into Castle House, Listerdale. By the end of 1924 Joe was a substantial landowner and his total holding at that point amounted to over 300 acres. Surviving records reveal that by September 29th, 1924, twenty-one of the houses were occupied and were returning ground rents; by March 25th, 1927, all of the forty houses in 'Old Listerdale' were occupied and returning ground rents. The total subsidies that Joe had received for building these houses must have amounted to between £9,600 and £10,400 and would have covered much of the building costs.

This had undoubtedly been a good start in Joe's career as a property developer.

It had not all been plain sailing. Grants were paid direct from the Ministry of Health in 1922 and they could not come fast enough for Joe whose finances must have been stretched. In a letter dated May 22nd, 1922, addressed to 'The Secretary, Ministry of Health' and headed 'Grants to private persons' he gives away his anxiety to receive the grant on three houses which had just been completed:

> Owing to the number of letters, pathetic and otherwise, chiefly otherwise, received by me from my bankers I have come to the conclusion that they are almost as hard up as I am, if such a position is possible, and consequently if you could let me have your remittance of £780 against the certificate of the 8th inst by an early post it would materially strengthen the quotations on the Exchange for The National Prov. and Union Shares as my overdraft with them would have been reduced by the above amount.

Joe was a man who felt passionately about many things and none more so than the welfare of his beloved housing estate. The road from Rotherham through Maltby and on to Bawtry had improved very little over the years before Joe bought any land in the area. It was obvious that it would not be able to cope with the increasing motor traffic from the 1920s onwards as well as the trolleybus or 'trackless' system of public transport which operated along the road running past the estate. Joe realised that efficient public transport was essential to any development at Listerdale and in the 1920s the estate could not be viable without it; the massive expansion in private car ownership was then years ahead and certainly not foreseen by many. As early as June, 1926, he wrote to the Chairman of Rotherham

Tramways Committee suggesting a series of 'electrically worked signals that light up say half a mile in front of the Trackless as it approaches and automatically shut off as it passes' to inform waiting passengers of its imminent arrival. He also campaigned for a better shelter for passengers, cheekily suggesting that 'there would [then] not be so many people wandering about suffering from loss of memory' which he put down to his belief that 'the poor devils originally were waiting in this shelter for a Trackless until their thinking apparatus froze stiff', and made the obvious point that as the shelter faced south west it was open to the prevailing winds. He suggested a simple remedy of filling the front with glass and fitting the doorway on the other side. In the same letter he claimed that he had an idea that would enable the driver of the trackless vehicle to operate in fog but did not elaborate on it beyond claiming that the patent for it would be 'worth thousands', and simply requested that the Committee, if they took up his idea, should merely tell his bank manager so 'that in future when he feels like giving me Hell about my overdraft he Puts a Sock in it'.

Joe could clearly see the problems with the main road that ran past his estate and as early as 1921 had sold a six hundred yard long strip of his newly acquired land to Rotherham Rural District Council, the highway authority at the time, for the purpose of road widening. Nothing happened. The road was eventually taken over by the West Riding County Council in 1923 and still nothing happened. Joe was incensed and sent several letters to both Councils demanding to know when the road would be widened complaining that the uncertainty was blighting the properties he was building adjacent to the road but still nothing happened and Joe finally decided at the end of 1925 that he had had enough. By January, 1926, travellers along the road were greeted by large hoardings, all of them headed 'LISTERDALE' and carrying the following messages:

More accidents might speed up
This road widening.
Motorists. be British and
Please oblige.
Phones for ambulances
Free on the estate.
****
Fellow beer drinkers
If this road were widened
You would have more to stagger on.
Why pay tax on beer?
****
Noah did not build his ark here
Because he could not get the animals up this road two abreast.

The second notice is ironic considering that Joe was a strict teetotaller and unsurprisingly Rotherham Rural District Council took great exception to them all, pointing out in a letter to Joe, which was printed in part in the *Sheffield Mail* of January 8th, 1926, that they were no longer the relevant highway authority as the road in question was a main road and that Joe should 'publicly state...that no reflection was intended [by him] on this Council'. The newspaper also reports that Joe had generously commented that if the West Riding County Council 'have any reply or explanation for the delay, he is quite willing to let them put up a counter-notice beside his own'. An undated cutting has survived, tucked into one of Joe's pocket diaries, which indicates that he took his campaign somewhat further. The item could be from a local newspaper for it is headed 'Mr. Lister's Latest' and it reports that he had been repeating his criticisms of West Riding County Council in the columns of *The Autocar*. There is a humorous sting in the tail of Joe's comments: 'Having just paid £47 road tax for the present year it is a pleasure to realise that this may be used by Mr. Winston Churchill [Chancellor of the Exchequer] for the roads of Iraq'. It was to be well after Joe's lifetime that the road was eventually widened and, ironically, it took quite a large proportion of Joe's own garden to turn it into the dual carriageway that is familiar to motorists on the route today.

Joe's campaign for the widening of Bawtry Road

CHAPTER NINE:

'A PERFECT LITTLE ARCADIA'

Photographs taken soon after Joe had begun his development of the older part of Listerdale show an almost treeless landscape with bungalows set in empty gardens and it takes considerable imagination to connect it with the leafy suburb into which it has now grown. The new and raw-looking estate is pictured standing next to a narrow single carriageway road which appears totally traffic free, worlds away from the busy dual carriageway that the same thoroughfare, Bawtry Road, has subsequently become. Joe's building operations literally became the 'talk of the town' at the time, with the *Rotherham Advertiser* carrying a somewhat pretentious article under the heading, 'Round and About Rotherham' by 'Vulcan' on January 24th, 1925, dealing with the expansion of house building that was going on at the time in the whole area. The unknown author certainly wishes to impress the public with his erudition for he even manages to find a way of including in the feature numerous references to figures from classical history, such as Caesar, Scipio and Seneca, and confidently forecast that forty years hence the centre of Rotherham would consist of 'palatial buildings' and 'imposing squares'; but it reserved most of its comment for Listerdale, although, curiously, Joe Lister himself is not mentioned by name throughout the whole of the long article, but is simply referred to as 'a son of Rotherham'. Listerdale is regarded as a triumph of private enterprise, 'the brightest local example of what private enterprise is doing towards providing "homes fit for heroes to live in"', and concludes with a ringing

**Two views of Listerdale in 1925.
Joe's bungalow is on the far right of the
lower picture**

declaration that it had a bright future before it. From
the article, however, we can catch a glimpse of the bold
vision Joe entertained for his estate as a community
even at this very early stage of its development, with the

spirit of 'Old Joe' invoked towards the end of the feature:

> "Listerdale" represents the worthy attempt of the third
> generation of the local Lister family to improve upon the efforts
> – Lister Street and Oxford Street are typical examples – of two
> predecessors to provide something better to live in than "brick
> boxes with slate lids". When completed with its communal
> laundry, communal traffic, etc., the lesson of "Listerdale" will be
> obvious. Could he have seen it, "Old Joe Lister" would have
> been proud of his progeny. Neither public nor private
> enterprise has done what is being done at "Listerdale" and
> what is really gratifying to know is that it is being done by a son
> of Rotherham, who has not only designed the estate but has
> been the architect of the houses.

Joe's enterprise did, however, attract attention from
other interesting and wider sources with the *Country
Illustrated* of April, 1925, devoting its leading feature to
Listerdale. The magazine, which described itself as 'a
monthly journal for all interested in country life and the
countryside', was published in London but this
particular edition carried a great deal of information on
Rotherham. The photograph on the cover is captioned
"Listerdale" and shows an expanse of valleys, hills and
woods, but no houses. It is in fact the land behind Joe's
development which he had bought when he purchased
his first farms and which was to provide recreation
ground for the occupiers of the houses he was building;
it included a natural bathing pool which is depicted on
the first inside page of the magazine. Joe had spent
£200 on the construction of bathing pools along the
Dalton Brook for the sole use of Listerdale residents and
objected when the pools were used by others without
permission, suggesting that the Council use some money
to make other pools lower down the brook 'to encourage
the development of swimming and at the same time

Swimming in the Denes at Listerdale

enable the users, who in a great many cases have no baths at home, to indulge their spirit of cleanliness'. The leading article in the magazine is entitled '"Listerdale" Calling' and like the *Rotherham Advertiser* it places the name within quotation marks which is very interesting, for although Joe from a very early date was freely using the name he had invented for his estate, it is an indication that the editors of both journals could not yet accept it as the official description of the area, a question that would trouble Joe more than once as he fought to establish recognition of his estate and the name he gave to it. The article is anonymous but the accompanying photographs are 'By courtesy of J. C. Lister, Esq.', and the entire article is lyrical in its appreciation of the development:

> If you know Rotherham but cursorily you will not imagine
> that within a stone's throw of it there is a perfect little Arcadia.
> Yet, there is. While the blast furnaces belch their smoke over
> Rotherham and the trams rattle their way through dreary files

of factories, to Sheffield, there lies, actually quite close (2.25 miles from Rotherham and 4.5 miles from the extensive works in the East end of Sheffield) yet hundreds of miles away so far as conditions are concerned, an Arcadia such as you and I dream of...

"Listerdale" is a private housing estate on that side of Rotherham that will eventually be its residential quarter...The country around here is glorious and a perfect sanctuary for the creatures of the wild – a typical beauty spot of old England. There could be no better place in which to plant health happy homes...

The owner of "Listerdale" is Mr. J. C. Lister, who is well-known in Rotherham...Although quite a young man Mr. Lister is most business-like and enterprising, as is evidenced by his having the shrewdness and courage to open up his estate entirely on his own responsibility. Purchasing the place about four years ago, he devised the whole scheme himself, and so far he has designed every house on the estate, a fact that proves him to be an architect of considerable ability and unusual resource.

The article continues by informing readers that Joe's estate as envisaged would eventually provide about a thousand homes and states that houses could be purchased from prices of £400 to £700 'on the most favourable terms'. The information concerning the projected size of the estate must have come from Joe himself and is a clear indication of the extent to which his ambition had grown by 1925. No-one seems to have thought to question whether there would be a market for that number of owner-occupied homes on the outskirts of Rotherham in the 1920s and if the development were to continue at the density of four houses to the acre it would need a total of 250 acres of land on which to build. When all the development of Listerdale eventually came to an end there were certainly over six hundred houses. Most of them, however, were built for letting to tenants rather than for sale to owner-occupiers and at a closer density of about twelve houses to the acre. Joe had never been trained as an architect, and in fact he did not, at the time, claim to be a professional builder, but to assist him there were various pattern books easily available, and a steady stream of them had appeared since well before the 1850s, all of which showed ready-made plans and elevations. He would undoubtedly have had access to the Government's *Housing Manual* of 1919, which included the Tudor Walters recommendations (see Appendix, pp 191-192), and he would have been able to consult a very useful periodical, the *Illustrated Carpenter and Builder*. Both of these publications carried standardised plans of house design, but many of the ideas incorporated in his housing scheme were undoubtedly his own and this meant that he was sometimes in trouble with the authorities. Occasionally, Joe's prospective purchasers had their own ideas for the design of the houses they hoped to buy from him. One in particular sent Joe a plan via the solicitors, Oxley and Coward, which included a proposal for five doors in the living room. Joe made short work of this idea in his reply:

> When I have to design houses with 5 doors out of the Living Room I'll give up building and start hair-pin bending. That of my own design has only two doors out of the Living Room, neither of which are outside doors and the Living Room fire cooks the oven in Scullery, furthermore the scullery is adjacent to bath room thereby improving the Hot Water Supply making the Plumbing and Sanitation more efficient.

Lead was the material commonly used for the flashing on the roofs of houses at the time Joe was building his estate and, although it is extremely durable, it has the disadvantage of being both heavy and expensive. A few years before Joe's building operations began, a new felt-based material, treated with bitumen and called 'Ruberoid', came on to the market as a substitute for lead and was approved for use in housing by the Ministry of Health in 1920. Joe used a small amount of Ruberoid in four of the houses he was building and it led to spirited correspondence with officials from Rotherham Rural District Council. The involvement of the Council was all the more significant because it was, by 1925, paying out the subsidy, or at any rate part of it, on behalf of the Government. In October, 1925, Joe received a letter from the Council demanding the removal, within twenty-one days, of the Ruberoid from the roofs of the four houses in question and its replacement with lead sheeting or, as he was informed, they would take proceedings against him, and, in any case, the payment of the subsidy would be withheld until Joe complied. It would have cost him very little to have met the Council's request but, never one to be pushed around by bureaucracy, Joe flatly refused, visited the Ministry in London in an attempt to obtain a ruling from them and then mounted a spirited campaign to get his way. He pointed out that the Ministry of Health regulations, and even the Council's own bye-laws, simply stated that the material to be used in roofing was to be 'incombustible' and did not specify lead to the exclusion of all other materials, even though the Council had wrongly done so in its letter to him, in contravention of their own bye-laws, he contended. His letter was laid before the Council through his solicitors, Oxley and Coward, but he was informed in a letter dated December 9th from the same solicitors that the Council believed 'it was undesirable to create a precedent by granting a subsidy in respect of houses being erected at the present date where Ruberoid as adopted by you is substituted for lead'. The Council recognised that Joe had built a good number of houses by this time and regretted the difficulty that had arisen but reminded him that he should not have continued with the use of Ruberoid after the Council's engineer had informed him that it would not be allowed. 'You should, therefore, within four weeks complete the work to Mr. Rawstron's [the Council's engineer] satisfaction if you wish to receive the subsidy'. In his answering letter to the Clerk of the Council dated December 18th, 1925, Joe threw the whole question back in their faces:

> If your Byelaws are so sacrosanct I fail to realise how it has come to pass that they have been so flagrantly molested in <u>each and every house</u> built and building since the War by such as Cortonwood, Dalton Main, Maltby Main and Rothervale Collieries and if you can show me any one house built by your own Council, by your own Architect, that complies with your existing Byelaws I will give £20 to Rotherham Hospital.
> It may or may not interest you to know that houses now being built by the thousand for such as Sheffield, Birmingham, Bradford and Leicester Corporations could not be built according to your Byelaws, nor could those at Eastdene for the Rotherham Corporation at a cost of £900 to £1000 each, built in pairs and fours and so finely balanced that gas cannot be used in them for illumination purposes and whereas mine all standing separately and sold at prices of £400 to £650 each can use either or both Gas and Electricity for Lighting... Some of the Subsidies I am entitled to have been withheld for months and it is very poor consolation to have the Bailiffs in the House distraining for Income Tax (which I have at the time of writing)...

His last comment shows how the whole issue of the payment of subsidy had become so critical for Joe whose building operations, carried out at this time on very tight margins, were stretching him almost to breaking point.

His pocket diary for February, 1926, contains a pencilled draft of a question that was obviously intended for the House of Commons:

> Is the Government aware that subsidy is being withheld by the Rotherham Rural District Council because 4 square feet only of the roof is composed of Ruberoid whereas other Councils have granted subsidy on houses roofed completely with Ruberoid?

He followed this up by writing to two MPs with a request that they raise the question on the floor of the House of Commons. They were not his local representatives and in his letter to one of them, Commander Kenworthy MP, he apologises for his 'effrontery' in approaching him rather than the MP for Rotherham and points out that he is doing so because 'there are members and Members'. In his letter to T. W. Grundy MP, he reveals that the whole issue has caused him to shut down his building operations 'until the question is settled'.

He went to some lengths to prove the incombustible nature of Ruberoid by inviting a reporter from the *Sheffield Mail* to witness a demonstration whereby he dropped a live coal on to a piece of the material. The reporter conceded in an item in the newspaper of January 8th, 1926, that: 'the glowing coal went black and died down without having any inflammatory effect on the "Ruberoid". "There!" exclaimed Mr Lister triumphantly, "That proves my point. If a live coal lying flat on the stuff does not fire it, what possible chance is there of a sloping roof coming to any harm from sparks or anything?"' The Rotherham newspapers took up the story the next day and gave it full coverage, with the

Rotherham Star quoting Joe's parting shot: 'If some one from time to time had not had the courage of his convictions, what few there would have been alive today would still be living in caves!'. Ruberoid eventually became a common feature of house-building which no doubt gave Joe enormous satisfaction.

Problems with the Inland Revenue were a recurring theme at this early stage of his development. In September, 1929, the local Inspector of Taxes wrote to Joe reminding him that he had not made a tax return for two years and pressed him for details of his profits from the building operations: 'a statement should be rendered by you shewing the amount of your earnings and expenditure, including bank interest for each of the years to 31st March or 5th April since you commenced developing the estate...'. His job at Joseph Green's provided him with a steady income on which it would be reasonably easy to assess the tax liability, but income from building is notoriously erratic. On the day he submitted his 1927 tax return, December 7th, he wrote a letter of complaint to the Inland Revenue:

> As reported to you some years ago the sole development of my estate was to create Ground Rents which at the present time amount to 40 @ £7 each from which 4/- in the £ is deducted at source and as my lawyers will only advance money on agricultural land values until such time as the value has appreciated I am obliged to borrow money (how and when) to carry out road making, sewers, mains, etc., hence my overdraft at the Bank the interest on which I most certainly consider should be set off against your income Tax on above Ground Rents.

While on the subject of rebate I think you have taxed me on a £500 bonus I have never had, i.e. that for Mch. 1925 to Mch 1926 year salary from Joseph Green, Rotherham, and should be glad if you would look into this...

I realise fully that my affairs could be dealt with more expeditiously by myself so far as you are concerned but as J Green has first call on my services, when I arrive home on many occasions I don't care a ------ for any further effort on my part, hence delay.

Earning money to pay His Majesty's Government seems to occupy too much of my time for me to be classed among the Idle Rich.

Soon after Joe had commenced building his houses the country began to experience a period of deflation and he argued some time later that his tax assessment should take account of this. It was in a letter he wrote to the Editor of the *Rotherham Star* on December 12th, 1928, explaining that he had earlier pointed out to the Inland Revenue that the cost of building was falling 'year by year and that which was £550 then could be erected for £525 the next year, £500 the year later and so on'. He maintained that in such circumstances the rent received should not be all counted as income but a portion of it should be regarded as a return of capital – 'if a house then built for £550 could be built for £450 say in 6 years then the owner should be able to treat £17 per year as a return of capital'. It will come as no surprise that the Inland Revenue would not agree to Joe's interesting piece of 'creative accounting' and he informed the Editor that 'if houses have not been built privately to let at as rapid a rate as the situation calls for this may be taken as one of the reasons...only fools would build to let under such conditions'.

The older part of Listerdale was completed by 1929 and Joe could see in later years how much he owed to this first venture in property development. He recorded his gratitude in a later comment when his estate had grown and hoped he would be in a position to reduce the ground rent of £7 a year as he now turned his attention to developing land on Brecks Farm which he had bought in the meantime. It consisted of about 70 acres and he had negotiated a price of £3,100 which had been financed by a mortgage arranged by his solicitors, Oxley and Coward. At Easter, 1929, he commenced building twenty houses in Brecks Lane which runs down to join the main road near the Brecks Hotel. These were smaller houses than those in 'Old Listerdale', and were built as semi-detached dwellings at a density of about eight to the acre. Subsidies in the meantime had been reduced and Joe obtained £100 per house from the Exchequer and sold the houses leasehold for £390 each with a ground rent of £3 per annum to take account of the smaller plot.

David Lloyd George had been forced to resign as Prime Minister in October, 1922, when the Conservatives decided to withdraw their support for his coalition. This change to a Conservative Government brought Neville Chamberlain to the Ministry of Health and he produced yet another Housing Act in 1923. The first ever Labour Government was elected in 1924 and only lasted a few months as it was in a minority in the House of Commons but its Minister of Health was John Wheatley who extended the provisions of the 1923 Act and it was under the terms of the 'Wheatley Act' that Joe built his first houses for rent. John Wheatley's Act recognised the stark fact that the shortage of working-class houses was greater in 1924 than it was in 1919 despite the 'Addison' measures (see Appendix, pp 194-195). These various Acts were particularly designed to encourage private builders like Joe and introduced for the first time a subsidy to private landlords who were building for rent. Like the 'Addison' subsidy, this one proved to be short-lived for it was reduced in 1927 and it was planned to phase it out in completely in 1929 in favour of subsidies to local authorities alone in order to concentrate on slum clearance in the cities. In actual fact the Wheatley subsidy continued until 1933 as the economic crisis of 1931 meant a postponement of plans for slum clearances. Over 500,000 homes were built under the terms of the Wheatley Act.

The 'Chamberlain' and 'Wheatley' Acts must have been one of the incentives from which sprang the building of the large rented estate at Listerdale. What is very apparent is that Joe followed the subsidy, whether for the owner-occupied houses or the rented ones that he built. Both the Conservative and Labour Governments had seen that local authorities could not be relied upon to solve the continuing housing crisis without some help from the private sector, for the authorities' experience in building and managing large estates was, at that date, very limited. The Government also knew that rents would have to be set at a level most people could afford if their housing policies were to be in any way successful and the figure they finally arrived at was to set rents at eight shillings and sixpence (42.5p) a week, later reduced to seven shillings and ten pence (approximately 39p), with a subsidy on each house payable to the landlord of nine pound ten shillings (£9.50) per year, two pounds of which would be paid by the local authority and, furthermore, this subsidy was intended to continue for forty years.

One effect of the building of the older part of Listerdale followed by the houses in Brecks Lane was that the value of land in the whole area was substantially enhanced. Joe had paid for the services of gas and electricity to be laid along the main road and into his estate and, not surprisingly, he was anxious that other adjacent land owners were now discovering that they were in a position to benefit at his expense should they decide to develop the land they owned. To prevent that from happening, there was no alternative but to make attempts to purchase more of the adjoining land which led him at that point to enter into unsuccessful negotiations with the Warde-Aldam family, who were the lords of the manor of Wickersley and who consequently owned a considerable amount of land in the area, for the purchase of a long narrow field next to his new bungalow. They informed him that they did not wish to sell which put him in a difficult position. Would all the risks he had taken with his considerable borrowings result in others reaping the rewards as the value of their land increased? Not if he could help it, and it so happened that there were other landowners of fields near to his development which, if he could negotiate a successful purchase, would ensure that no-one else could carry out building which would be detrimental to his own scheme. One of these land owners was the Church of England in the guise of the Ecclesiastical Commissioners who owned the land beyond the Warde-Aldam field and Joe first purchased nine acres from them for £550 and then entered into protracted negotiations to purchase a further twenty one

Black Carr Road under construction

acres for £1,100. He finally did manage to complete the transaction but not before he had taken what must have been the greatest risk of all. As in 1921 with his 'Addison' subsidies, he was, in 1929, working very close to the point where all grants to private landlords were to be phased out. He had to start his building very quickly but he had not yet completed the purchase from the Commissioners. Despite this risky position, in February, 1930, he started to build houses in what now constitutes Springfield, Black Carr and Melciss Roads after encountering enormous difficulty in obtaining the necessary finance for the scheme. This cannot have been surprising for, in effect, he was building on land legally owned by others and if they had at the last minute decided not to sell after all, then the houses Joe was building would have become the property of the original landowner with Joe at great risk of losing every penny of his borrowings. Bankruptcy would undoubtedly have been the result but, happily, the sale went through as agreed.

This first part of his estate of houses for rent totalled one hundred houses. He followed it up a year later in 1931 by building seventy more houses in Brecks Crescent and a surviving fragment of pencilled accounts for the year ending 20th, February, 1931, indicates how much he was stretched in the financing of these building operations. He was highly 'geared', using borrowed money to establish the estate with no possibility, as the houses were to be let, of retrieving the capital for years to come, and the accounts reveal that he had by that time borrowed over £40,000, of which £33,000 was accounted for by the mortgages for the hundred houses he had so far built for letting. It was a very large debt for an individual in 1931 and at 2004 values it represents borrowings of nearly £2.25m, but it proved to be only a start. In a letter dated November 26th, 1930, and addressed to Mr Pickles of the solicitors, Oxley and Coward, he protests at their charges for professional services and estimates his income from all his property to be £4,170 per annum and his 'outgoing interest' payments to be £2,310, leaving him with a gross income of £1,860 'net income from Listerdale Estate'. He adds that £1,000 of this is being paid every year to the Building Society as a reduction of principal which left him with £860 per year 'which may be termed liquid'. Building houses for renting was a major departure from his original scheme of a private estate of owner-occupiers, whereby he was quickly able to recoup his initial investment (with a profit) when the houses were sold and then continue to receive ground rent, and Joe's new venture was an enormous gamble at a time of economic depression. He was paying interest, by no means fixed, of between 5 and 5.5 per cent and had no possibility of knowing whether this 'leap in the dark' was to lead to unmanageable debts or whether it was a shrewd and clever move in difficult and deflationary times. His position was saved by the Exchequer subsidy he was receiving which amounted to £950 a year on these early rented houses in Listerdale and, as it turned out, these initial hundred houses were only the first stages of a much larger undertaking.

Joe's houses which he was now building for rent would have been a great improvement on the cramped conditions under which so many of his tenants must have lived prior to moving to Listerdale. He was building right up to the Tudor Walters standard and his houses were of the three-bedroom semi-detached type with bathroom and a driveway to each property which ensured that each pair of houses was situated at a distance from its neighbour. The roads were built wide enough to allow sunlight to penetrate into the ground-floor rooms throughout the year and the houses were built to a density of approximately twelve to the acre, slightly more than was recommended by Tudor Walters for rural areas, but they benefited from being very close to open space which was intended for the use of all the tenants.

PART THREE: FROM TRAGEDY TO TRIUMPH

CHAPTER TEN:

A TIME OF SORROW

In early 1930 Joe and Mary Evelyne had been married for nearly sixteen years and Joe had every reason to be grateful to his wife. His pet name for her was 'Ciss' and he showed his gratitude for all her help and support, which had included using much of her savings to assist him at the start of his project, in an enduring way by naming one of the roads in the estate after her. 'Melciss Road' must be a unique name for a street and is made up of her initials with his pet name for her added as a suffix. There is further concrete evidence of Joe's affection for his family at the junction of Melciss and Dale Roads where there are houses which carry the initials, JCL, MEL, MGL, and CJL. Despite this proof of undoubted affection and gratitude he sometimes liked to pose as the hen-pecked husband and an example can be seen in a tongue-in-cheek letter of April 24th, 1923, written to the Davis Gas Stove Company Ltd, the most unlikely recipients of the surprising sentiments expressed about his wife. He was actually complaining about a bill he had received from them but opened with the following remarks:

> In order to lead a placid existence I have surrounded myself with all the work dodging appliances that are sprung upon an unsuspecting public at various times and even then I have to do such things as my own breathing and listen to a wife who would make a damned good Official Receiver by the manner she employs when lecturing me upon my shortcomings in dealing with correspondence, etc., so if future correspondence is headed

Mrs. you will realise that for the sake of peace and quietness I have handed over the reins of government to the opposition so that I may devote more time looking down the columns of the Daily Mail for self sacrificing wife who having fallen downstairs and broken her neck has increased the value of her husband's estate...

Those letters written by Joe which have survived contain few references to Mary Evelyne and nearly all are of a humorous nature but one gets the impression that, as in so many marriages of successful men, she was the unsung heroine of the story. Joe, as kind and generous as he was, could not have been an easy person to live with and as he expanded his estate, his preoccupation with it together with the financial worries that went along with this expansion tended to squeeze out any time he might have been able to spend with his family.

Joe needed to keep up to date with all the developments in the building trade during the period of the rapid expansion of his estate and where better than the Building Exhibition in London which took place in the early part of 1930? It was a splendid showcase for the construction industry and he drove there from Listerdale with Mary Evelyne. They had not been in London very long when she was suddenly taken ill and they had to drive back to Rotherham along the Great North Road, making their way home very promptly where Mary Evelyne took to her bed in an attempt to recover at home in the bungalow on Bawtry Road, but sadly there was no improvement. At the time they employed a maid who now took on the task of looking after Mary Evelyne during her illness, and on one occasion when she was on her way upstairs to answer

Mary Evelyne's hand-bell she noticed as she passed their cage that one of the two parrots that Joe had bought as household pets was shaking uncontrollably and lying at the bottom of the cage. When she arrived upstairs she discovered that Mary Evelyne had become feverish, shaking in exactly the same manner as the parrot and, rightly thinking there might be some connection, sent for the local doctor who admitted her to Clifton Lane Nursing Home in Rotherham where it was eventually diagnosed that the illness was psittacosis, commonly known in those days as 'parrot fever', a highly infectious pneumonic respiratory condition that is passed on to humans by birds. As its common name indicates, it is mostly associated with parrots but can, in fact, be caught from other birds such as pigeons and budgerigars. There was an epidemic of the disease in the 1930s and Mary Evelyne had undoubtedly caught it from the one of the parrots that Joe and she kept as pets. Psittacosis is a 'notifiable' disease involving the informing of the local health authority of each occurrence, and regulations were later introduced that prevented the keeping of parrots unless they were born and bred in Britain. This did not come in time to help the Lister family and within a few days Joe himself was taken ill with the same complaint. On Easter Saturday, April 19th, they were both admitted to Swallownest Isolation Hospital, which was situated on the road between Sheffield and Worksop, with Joe protesting that he wanted to be in the same ward as his wife but to no avail. In the 21st century, psittacosis can be easily treated with antibiotics, usually tetracycline, and does not often prove fatal, but in the 1930s medical knowledge was not advanced enough to deal with the problem and after a month Mary Evelyne tragically succumbed to the disease and died in the hospital on May 15th, 1930, while Joe was lying ill in another ward. She was only 42. For the family this was utterly devastating and, despite his own still quite serious condition, Joe refused to stay in hospital any longer and discharged himself the following day in order to make the necessary arrangements for his wife's funeral. It must have been extraordinarily difficult for him but he came through it and Mary Evelyne was buried in Wickersley Churchyard on May 19th. Bearing in mind that he was recovering from his own illness, and the fact that he was now left with two children aged 13 and 11, it must have been a shocking ordeal for him. It is remarkable that he made any sort of recovery at all but he did and survived, forced as he was to face the fact that he was now a widower after less than sixteen years of marriage. Marjorie remembers her mother as a tall, slim and elegant lady who wore very pretty hats, a reflection no doubt on her early training as a milliner.

Almost immediately after his admission to hospital Joe put pen to paper and produced an (unfinished) statement of his affairs 'financial and otherwise' because of 'an element of doubt existing as to the immediate future'. The document, dated 'Easter Monday, April 21st,' is handwritten on foolscap paper, is addressed 'To whom it may concern' and details the history of his land acquisitions and building operations to that date. Each page is signed 'Joseph C. Lister' and it was obviously intended to be some form of last will and testament hurriedly drawn up to assist any executor should Joe himself succumb to his illness. It is a remarkably detailed document for someone writing whilst suffering from a very acute illness and he must have had the relevant papers to hand or he had a phenomenal memory for the purchase prices and acreages of land he had bought, as well as the selling prices of many of the houses he had built, including accounts of the money still owing upon some of them. Later in that same year, on October 21st, he produced another handwritten document addressed 'To My Children or to whom it may concern'. This was both signed by him on every page and witnessed by two other signatories, both from Listerdale. In it he makes quite clear that he had borrowed substantially from Mary Evelyne to help finance his building operations at Listerdale and that he had endeavoured to pay her back, but there was still an amount of £200 owing to her when she died. As the cash had not been readily available during her lifetime he had given her the Willys Knight car which is why, he informed his children, their mother always regarded the Willys Knight as her own. Mary Evelyne had left £500 left in the bank when she died which Joe promised to put into an account held in the names of his children, Clifford and Marjorie, and himself, in order that they might have access to money should he die. This, he declared, was in accordance with their mother's wishes.

It is hard to discover just how deeply Joe was affected by Mary Evelyne's death. He was a driven man as far as his estate of Listerdale was concerned and the burdens of his immense borrowings always weighed heavily upon him knowing that if he ever came to the point of being unable to service these debts the whole enterprise would collapse like a pack of cards. Later in the 1936 account of his life he admitted somewhat wistfully how all this must have affected his wife who never lived to see much of the benefit of his enterprise:

I realize the tragedy of [my children's] lives in losing their mother while so young. I also realize where my being the husband might have led to more pleasure in my wife's life, but being so wrapped up in carrying out the projects of the moment, I was inclined to treat what to my wife were major worries, as minor ones and I am afraid I did not give her the consideration she was entitled to.

Joe had noticed during his stay in the isolation hospital how difficult it was for relatives and friends who were visiting patients owing to the lack of an adequate place for them to wait until they could be admitted to the wards where they could even then only see patients under the strictest conditions. They had to wait outside the hospital until the time for admission. Even though his finances were stretched he was able to arrange for enough money to be made available for the building of a waiting room and after Mary Evelyne's death and his own discharge from hospital he donated the waiting room to enable visitors to wait their turn in comparative comfort. It was out of his gratitude for the hospital's attempts to save his wife and is an early example of his generosity which later became legendary.

How was Joe to manage to bring up two young children on his own? It was an impossible task with the building of his estate then in full swing and the consequent increase in the demands on his time outside the home. Joe's family came to the rescue. His brother, Donald, had married a Welsh girl called Myfanwy and they came to live with Joe and his family in the bungalow, bringing their own son, Ian, with them. Myfanwy performed the duties of housekeeper and surrogate mother to both Marjorie and Clifford but she was always known as Megan, perhaps on account of the difficulties in pronouncing Welsh names in South Yorkshire. Ian well remembers those days and recalls how the whole family came over from Wales to live at the Castle as a temporary measure, intending to stay just 'for a fortnight' to help Joe over a difficult period, but this arrangement stretched for much longer and continued until 1941 when they moved into a nearby bungalow which had been built by Joe on Bawtry Road. On 12th December, 1940, while they were still living at the Castle they all took shelter from the Sheffield blitz in the cellar.

When they first arrived at the Castle the building was not finished and Ian vividly remembers as a child being carried up a ladder to bed. He saw very much of his uncle Joe during that time as his own father, Joe's brother, Donald, was a member of the Territorial Army and was called up in 1938, serving until 1945. Life could have its exciting moments for a young lad at the Castle in those days and Ian remembers the moment when a religious enthusiast turned up at the back door with a small clockwork gramophone containing a recorded religious message. The caller insisted on playing it, despite Megan's protests, whereupon Joe made an even stronger protest and put his foot through the machine, completely wrecking it. Ian remembers Joe then marched across the yard with the spring wound round his leg.

In 1935 a maid, Annie Powell, was employed and stayed with the family for a long time taking on many duties, particularly in wartime, and in 1944 when the Rotherham Employment Exchange wanted to direct her into war work, Joe wrote to them pleading for her to be allowed to stay at Listerdale as the running of the estate meant that someone had to be at home in Castle House to deal with all the enquiries from tenants:

> At the outbreak of war I had housekeeper, two staff and daughter to deal with these matters and since that time, two staff have joined women's sections [of the services], the daughter is married (husband in Africa) and has a daughter 13 months old…and Powell is now the only one to give assistance.
>
> She has been with me for 8/9 years and her experience here enables her to deal most effectively with most items, but this ability does not always permit her giving an eye to the child, answering callers at the door and telephone at the same time, my daughter when necessity arises doing farm work, tractor driving, etc. as I am farming two farms myself, which adds to the work to be carried out here.
>
> Matters are not made easier by the A.R.P. [Air Raid Precautions] using part of the house for their head quarter report post and to my mind I think any probable help she could give to the war effort elsewhere would be far less in this respect than her services here.

Ian remembers that it was at this point, 1944, that Joe's health was failing and he and his family then moved back into the Castle as his mother was needed to nurse him during these times. He was suffering from dreadful headaches, possibly migraine, and needed complete rest and quiet during those periods.

Mary Evelyne's tragic death had the effect of making Joe even more remote from his family. His was now a single-parent family and his business concerns took up an enormous amount of his time and energy. Marjorie remembers that her father used to relax in the evenings by doing crosswords and that sometimes he would call out to her for an answer to one of the clues. There was very little ordinary conversation and at ten o'clock in the evening he would snap his fingers, which was sign that he was ready for his evening drink of Ovaltine or Cocoa and that it had to be provided for him immediately. Marjorie also remembers that on one occasion when she was ill her father never came to see her as he was far too busy. There were, however, happy holidays at Bridlington and there are photographs in the family collection showing them all enjoying themselves together, usually surrounded by many others, even strangers, whom Joe had invited on the spur of the moment to join in the fun.

Joe became very conscious of the little time he was able to spend with his children and referred to this in his 1936 account hoping they would eventually understand:

> If my children compare me to fathers of other children they know, I dare say from the actual fatherly interest I take in them, I do not show to advantage; but I think when they realize in years to come just what the culmination point of my present worries, and shall we say – slight interest in them has led up to – they will perhaps realize that what they might consider somewhat of an injustice at the present moment, or lack of attention on my part, is more than compensated for by the position I leave them in.

CHAPTER ELEVEN:
A CHANGE OF COURSE

In addition to the acreage he had bought from the Ecclesiastical Commissioners, Joe had bought three farms in the parishes of Dalton and Wickersley and by 1930 was the owner of a great amount of land which was of no use to him unless more houses were built on enough of it to produce a return on the capital invested. Government subsidies for houses built for sale were long discontinued and it looked as if subsidies for houses built by private enterprise for rent were going the same way, as the Government under Ramsay MacDonald wished to concentrate on slum clearance in the cities, which was to be carried out by the local authorities. Joe had always followed the subsidy and it looked as if he might now be coming to the end of that particular road with what might turn out to be dire consequences for his life's work. Council housing appeared to be taking over from private enterprise but there was one factor that worked in Joe's favour. Whereas large city local authorities could command the resources to build the large inter-war estates that are still to be seen across the country, smaller local authorities such as Rotherham Rural District Council would be struggling to cope with demand.

At this point Joe took a remarkable initiative in writing to the Prime Minister. He gave Ramsay MacDonald the benefit of his experiences in negotiating with the 'prominent building societies of this district' and listed the results he had obtained from those negotiations. His argument was that it was impossible for the private builder to compete with the local authorities 'so long as he had to pay the high rates of interest and obtain the low valuations which were then being granted by the building societies'. It meant that the private developer was required to find far too much finance on his own account as the societies were not prepared to lend enough for any scheme to go ahead. The actual letter has not survived, nor has any reply, but Joe gives his own account of what happened next:

> Within a few days, I visited the Ministry of Health by appointment, with Mr. Cloke of the Housing Committee of the Rotherham Rural District Council, and the treasurer, and whilst talking to Mr. Kerwood, the man who dealt with our area, mention was made of the letter I had sent to the Prime Minister. Mr. Kerwood said the letter had been handed on to him and they were very impressed with the suggestions made and were prepared to give my scheme a trial. The representatives of the Rotherham Rural District Council were told that the section of the Act dealing with advances by the Building Societies of 90% to owner occupiers and guaranteed by the Council could, as an experiment in my case, be read as for houses also built to let.

Joe was overjoyed at this turn of events which meant that he now could borrow a larger amount of the finance necessary for the development he had in mind, as he knew by now that he had to change course and that there was not, in 1931, a large enough market in the Rotherham area for the building of a large estate of houses for sale. The country was, after all, in the middle of a very serious economic depression which had started with the stock market fall on Wall Street, New York, in 1929, and his only hope was to find himself in a position whereby he could continue building houses for rent and make the project pay. For this he would need a continuation of the subsidy and the result of his meeting in London meant that he had now, uniquely, achieved that. All the controversy over the use of Ruberoid seems to have been forgotten as he now entered into discussions with the Council as to how he should proceed. In fact, he was doing the Council an enormous favour as they were under pressure, like all local authorities, to build more and more houses to resolve the ongoing housing crisis. They were one of the smaller authorities with few resources and Joe's enterprising nature and his willingness to face risks could not have come at a more convenient time for them.

His enthusiasm seemed to have run away with him at this point for he immediately agreed to build a thousand houses under his new scheme but this frightened a somewhat reluctant Rotherham Rural District Council. They thought it was far too ambitious and wanted him to build a hundred and see how it all went. If everything was carried out to the Council's satisfaction with the first batch of houses Joe could make a further application and the Council would then perhaps allow the building of another hundred and this procedure would continue until a total of four hundred was reached. Joe was having none of this and pointed out that, according to the Government's regulations, the scheme was a temporary experiment giving him only twelve months in which to complete it. By dint of argument and persuasion he managed to convince them that it would be impossible for him to build and finish one hundred and repeat the performance every three months until the total of four hundred houses were completed in a year. In the 1930s it took more than three months to build a house from start to finish and the Council finally took the point, giving Joe permission to start the building of the four hundred houses immediately. Two hundred and fifty of these houses now stand on Rosemary Road, Green Lane, part of Black Carr and Springfield Roads and the extension to Melciss Road. The other one hundred and fifty are at a little distance away in the parish of Dalton and comprise part of Toll Bar Road, Brecks Crescent and Gibbing Greaves Road. When the building operations were finished, Joe was receiving subsidies on 598 houses and, at £9.50 per year for each dwelling, this amounted to a total of £5,681 every year and was intended to continue for forty years. It is difficult to assess his total income from the rents for these houses as there was some element of variation between a maximum rent of eight shillings and sixpence per week (42.5p) and a slightly lower one of seven shillings and ten pence (38p approximately) but if it is averaged out at 40p a week (in modern currency) he was receiving around £12,500 per year from the rents which, together with his subsidy, makes a total annual income before tax of approximately £18,100. Out of this total he would have to pay the rates on the properties as the rents were 'compounded' (i.e. they included rates) and any running repairs which became necessary, which were not likely to have been heavy as the properties were new. Later, in 1934, Joe obtained permission to build a further 50 houses, this time without subsidy, at some distance away from his earlier estate of rented housing. These were slightly larger and were built on the area known as The Brow. The rent on these was fixed at a higher rate of twelve shillings and sixpence (62.5p) per week and would add a further £1625 to his gross income from rented property bringing it to nearly £20,000 per annum, before the payment of interest on his debts and before tax. This was a very respectable return on his investment but an indication of just how financially stretched he was at this point can be discovered from his 1936 account where he records that the ground rents which he created on the older part of Listerdale, 40 properties at £7.00 per annum, had to be mortgaged in order to raise more money for the development of the estate and he admits 'that it was only by making extensive use of borrowed money that I have become the owner of so much property', a clear example of what is now called 'gearing', the use of money raised by borrowing to create an income, and relying on that income to be greater than the interest that must be paid to service the debts. He adds 'in passing' that had he built just 100 houses to let he would have had less cause for worry. Looking back from the vantage point of the 21st century, the 1930s appear a to have been very stable time but that could not have been so for those who were living through it and taking gigantic risks with money that they did not own. There is the old advice of never dabbling in the stock market with borrowed money. Joe risked little in stocks and shares but he was always at risk of being wiped out completely in the event of a property crash, or if interest rates should rocket to highly prohibitive levels. There are stories that he told people he never slept, although he never mentions sleepless nights in any of the records he has left behind, but his financial situation must have caused him a considerable number and his children always remembered how pre-occupied he was with his business concerns.

There is an interesting footnote to his correspondence with Ramsay MacDonald. In September, 1932, MacDonald's daughter, Jean, married Dr. Alastair MacKinnon of Edinburgh who had Wickersley connections. Joe sent them a present and among his papers is a letter of thanks from Jean MacDonald sent from 10 Downing Street, where Ramsay MacDonald remained as Prime Minister of the National Government after the severe economic crisis of 1931. It is dated September 15th and, after acknowledging that Joe had already been invited to the wedding by her future husband, Alastair, she includes her own invitation to the event by adding, 'As the printed invitations have run out I hope you will forgive this written invitation'. The wedding, which was to be at Wendover Congregational Church on September 20th, was to be followed by a reception at Chequers, the prime ministerial country residence. These very personal invitations make it look very probable that Joe was not on the original list of those officially invited and may have been included as a result of his present to them. Along with the letter is the calling card of Dr. MacKinnon with an added inscription on the reverse, 'Dear Mr. Lister, Please bring Marjorie along with you, Yours sincerely, Alastair U. MacKinnon'. Marjorie was fifteen at the time and well remembers the event. She visited Cockayne's, then a fashionable shop in Sheffield, and bought a new outfit for the occasion before travelling by car with her father to the wedding at the Congregational Church followed by the reception which was held in a marquée on the lawn at Chequers. It was all very interesting to her except for the fact that it rained.

Joe's burgeoning enterprise following his letter to Ramsay MacDonald must have been a godsend to much of Rotherham at a time when the dole queues stretched along the pavement. He employed 450 people to complete his estate over that year, providing much needed income for many families who would have been dependent upon unemployment pay had Joe not had the courage and foresight to take on the Government and the Council. Many of those who made up his workforce would have been casual labourers anxious for any job in those difficult days but some stayed for a considerable time with him. One of them, 'Jock' Robson, would often recall his first day in Joe's employment. He had come down from Scotland looking for work and, upon arriving in Rotherham, had picked up the information that Joe Lister was setting men on. Jock arrived on site and the first thing he saw was Joe reversing at break-neck speed down the muddy road shouting at the workmen, 'Come on, you buggers, these houses are not going up bloody fast enough'. Jock declared that he would not be staying as he didn't believe in swearing. He stayed, became a good friend to Joe Lister, a loyal member of staff and could still be seen climbing roofs well into his seventies.

The benefits of his scheme spread much further as he was providing work for those firms and undertakings that supplied him with the materials for his building operations. Joe was on good terms with many of them and they were prepared to give him extended credit in order for him to complete the estate. There were, however, times when their patience was stretched. One of his suppliers, a builders' merchant called George Friend Taylor of Greasborough wrote on 13th July, 1932, obviously replying to a proposal put forward by Joe:

> At present you hold – unsecured and unacknowledged – about one quarter of my Capital, which is also my only life

insurance...However, not being either a Banker nor a Steelmaker, but a gambler who has previously lost and won, I am prepared to accept your scheme in principle, to the following limits.

The balance due on last year's contracts together with goods supplied to June 30th, is roughly £2000.

Assuming goods to be supplied to be £750 per month, then you will owe me £3500 on August 31st.

Therefore – you issue a bill, or a cheque for £1000 payable August 31st, a further one for the same amount for September 30th, and in each successive month, a ditto to cover the outstanding balance, but leaving not more than £1000 to remain to the end of the job @ 6%.

The 'Wheatley' subsidy was to be phased out in 1929 and all houses built under its terms had to be completed by September 30th, 1930, which put Joe under enormous pressure. These houses were the first to be built by him for letting and amounted to a total of one hundred. He appealed to the Rotherham Rural District Council for some tolerance in a letter dated September 23rd, 1930, in which he complained that the weather had been extremely wet, causing a delay in all building operations over which, he pleaded, he had no control. He cites an example of bureaucratic delay:

I first wrote the Government about the scheme July last year but did not receive any authority to build until February last. Shortly after commencement, the wife and I were laid up with Psittacosis. I did not receive the deeds of the land until I was building the 64th house and owing to the delayed answer from Whitehall the Building Society held up a considerable payment for some time. Furthermore, the sanction for the last twenty was not given until the last week of July so I consider no reproach attaches to my efforts and trust you can agree to my request.

No record of the Council's reply exists and it is curious that he mentions his wife's illness but without any reference to the fact that she had died but he continued to develop his estate of subsidised housing to let and it can only be assumed that he came to an arrangement with the Council which enabled him to carry on.

After he commenced the estate of rented houses, Joe built no more for sale to owner-occupiers but as late as 1929 he was extolling the benefits of owning over renting in a publicity leaflet he issued advertising his building of houses for sale in Brecks Lane. In these leaflets he invoked the spirit of his grandfather, 'Old Joe', and they give no indication that he was about to embark on the large enterprise of building for rent. As the 1920s gave way to the 1930s, fewer people felt enough confidence in the future to risk buying a house but homes were still needed and more and more people were of the opinion that they would rather rent a property. Joe's vision of a 'perfect little Arcadia' of owner-occupied housing just could not be realised in the economic climate of the time and he had a great amount of land on his hands, bought with borrowed money where there was no prospect of a 'holiday' in servicing the debt. Unless he could develop the land it would remain a millstone round his neck and eventually cripple him financially as the prospect of re-selling it at a profit was non-existent. The large undertaking that Joe would now take on as a result of his agreement to build for Rotherham Rural District Council meant that he lived on the tightest of margins for the rest of his life. He was squeezed between controlled rents and fluctuating interest rates. It is then perhaps small wonder that he was moved to write on October 21st,

1930, in the document addressed 'To my children' that 'Listerdale Estate has caused me a lot of worry and for this reason I would like you to stick to it and carry it on as now most of the spade work has been done there should be both pleasure and profit out of it in the future'. The family has carried out Joe's wishes.

CHAPTER TWELVE:

A STATELY PROGRESS

Joe Lister, the son and grandson of Rotherham builders had hardly begun his own career as a builder and property developer when he had designs on becoming a country gentleman complete with a stately home and extensive parkland. As was the case with all his ventures at this stage, it could only be accomplished by money that he was able to borrow. Undeterred by the attendant risks he went ahead and managed to acquire an estate which came with a stately home which had, it is true, seen better days. It was only a few miles from Torworth where he and Mary Evelyne had set up their first home together and Joe had 'run a few fowls, pigs, etc.' and was in the village where their marriage had taken place in the summer of 1914.

Blyth Hall in Nottinghamshire was the home of the Mellish family from the 17th century until 1806 when they moved to nearby Hodsock Priory, now famous for its wonderful display of snowdrops in late winter, and Blyth was then acquired by Joshua Walker of Rotherham fame, one of the co-founders of the firm of Samuel Walker and Co. Later in the 19th century it came into the possession of Capt. Francis Willey who was eventually elevated to the peerage in 1922 as Lord Barnby, the title deriving from the nearby Barnby Moor. Their family fortune was based on the Bradford wool trade and when he died in 1929 he was succeeded by his son, Francis Vernon Willey, who was at the time making something of a name for himself as an expert in the wool textile industry. He is commemorated by a bronze tablet in the porch at Blyth Church for his munificence in paying for the restoration of the porch and south-west door of the church in memory of his parents in 1962, but his interests were not really in Nottinghamshire and he had no need of the property at Blyth which was promptly put up for sale on the death of his father.

Blyth Hall, Nottinghamshire (now demolished)

Blyth Hall had been a noble building and White's Directory of 1853 described it as being 'an elegant brick building decorated with stone and having turrets at the corners'. Blyth is an ancient and attractive village in north Nottinghamshire which looks more like a small market town with its broad central street where the market was once held. A Benedictine monastery was founded there in 1088, only a few years after the Norman Conquest, and its importance in medieval times can be appreciated by the fact that Blyth was one of the five places licensed by King Richard I (The Lionheart) for the holding of tournaments which took place on level ground between the village and its neighbour, Styrrup, some two miles away to the north-west. Blyth Hall was built on the site of the former monastic buildings but by 1929 it had fallen into a dilapidated state. The First World War seriously affected the landed estates of England as high taxation followed by an agricultural depression had eaten into many of the owners' ability to maintain them properly. When the Hall and its adjoining estate were put up for sale no-one came forward who was in a position to buy it in its entirety and consequently it was all sold piecemeal.

Joe's purchase of Blyth Hall is among the more curious of his transactions. He would have liked to have bought it in its entirety but could not raise the finance in time for that. Consequently, he was late coming into the picture and although he had purchased some of the fittings and furnishings, including the bed and wardrobe which was later to be the centrepiece of his own castle, by the time he had finance available much of the estate was in fact already sold to someone who lived in Exeter. However, Joe records that this particular purchaser 'had got into financial difficulties with his limited company, and Lloyds Bank of Exeter took over', so after considerable negotiation Joe was able to buy the site of the Hall together with its 'Lake and Grounds, Rock Garden Grounds and building plots' for £2,800. But this did not include the fabric of the Hall itself with its outbuildings and it is recorded that he paid a further £2,000 to enter into possession of the building which 'whilst not being habitable – was practically weather-proof', as Joe later described it. He adds somewhat ruefully, 'Had I been able to have obtained a satisfactory mortgage for half the amount of purchase, I could – and would have bought Blyth Hall [in its entirety] for £5000 but no-one seemed anxious to advance money on this large type of house'.

Blyth Hall Gates

The mention of 'building plots' in the record might indicate that he was thinking of developing the estate but this never happened and Joe could not even raise the necessary amount on the mortgage market to pay the vendors so the arrangement he finally arrived at with them was to pay back the purchase money at £500 per year plus interest; effectively, Lloyds Bank of Exeter advanced the money. Most of the large internal and external fittings had already been sold separately and it was with a great amount of difficulty that Joe was able to obtain any of them. He has left no conclusive evidence that he bought the Hall with the intention of living in the place, apart from the statement in his 1936 account that he had entertained dreams of preserving the building, but it proved to be beyond repair (or beyond his means to repair it) and many years later it was eventually demolished, although he was able to incorporate and preserve some of the internal features from the building in his own 'castle' at Listerdale.

The entrance gates of the Hall had been bought at the sale by a Doncaster auctioneer who was holding them for Lord Trent, otherwise known as Jesse Boot, the Nottingham chemist and founder of the Boots chain, who wanted to incorporate them in Trent College in Nottingham (now the University of Nottingham) which he had handsomely endowed from the profits of Boots the Chemist. Joe's persuasiveness worked and the auctioneer agreed to part with them for £150, Trent College having to do without them. The gates are still there in Blyth although the Hall has long since disappeared and in recent years a smart housing estate has been built on the site. The gates form an ornamental approach to the estate and are still complete with their carved gateposts. The purchase of the Hall was by no means the end of Joe's spending at Blyth as he bought the stables for £500 and the parkland around the Hall for £800 together with four cottages at the entrance to the Hall and three more cottages in the main street. On all these extra purchases he took out heavy mortgages and so became a major landowner and property owner in the village. Joe's list of his properties which he composed whilst in hospital on 23rd November, 1941, includes the property at Blyth:

> Blyth Hall, Stables, Grounds, Park, Lake and land across the Lake bought at various times from Bartletts (Stables and Main Gates were purchased from Fowler, Auctioneer, Doncaster, who bought them at the main Sale and sold them to me privately afterwards).
> Four Cottages at the main entrance to Blyth Hall.
> Three Cottages in the Main Street, Blyth.

In Clifford Lister's handwriting written after Joe's death is an added note, undated, to the effect that the Hall had been sold and was now demolished as were the three cottages in Main Street, but that 7 acres of parkland still remained in the ownership of Listerdale Estates.

Blyth Hall remained in Joe's ownership for the rest of his life and was finally sold by his family in 1950. It is hard to discover what advantage it held for him, apart from the rescue of some of its internal fittings and their subsequent use in Joe's own home, 'The Castle' at Listerdale. Even though it might have contained building plots, he could not possibly have bought it in 1930 with any thoughts of re-developing the site, as another housing estate as there was no adequate public transport serving the village at that time and car-ownership was not very widespread as it is today. The income he obtained from his Blyth transactions must have been meagre for it would consist solely of the rents on the seven cottages he owned in the village. There would have been no appreciable increase in its capital value at that time as land values were falling before the Second World War rather than rising and, as Joe had recognised, the Hall was not habitable. It must therefore have remained as something of a 'white elephant' for him and only added to his worries at the time. During the 1939-45 War it was requisitioned by the army. Joe opposed this requisitioning of his property but there survives among his papers a letter from the Quartering Commandant, No. 9 & 10 Areas and dated July 9th, 1942, insisting that the requisition must proceed.

However, he seemed determined to find himself a grand residence in addition to the one he was building at Listerdale, and the Blyth Hall estate had at one time included the Priory at Tickhill, a village close to Rotherham. This Priory had commenced its existence as a medieval foundation of Augustinian Friars, had been dissolved in 1537 at the Reformation, eventually being acquired by the owners of Blyth Hall when, on August 31st 1933, it was put up for sale by auction after a mortgage on the property was foreclosed. Joe bid successfully and obtained it for £2000 including its 13 acres of land and a cottage. He was now at last able to realise his ambition of occupying an ancient and historic property after he added a new wing and carried out a complete refurbishment. Tickhill Priory may not have been the country seat of Blyth Hall set in acres of parkland but it is a substantial house with many medieval features. It never became their permanent residence but Joe and the family used it as a weekend retreat, odd as that might seem as it was only a few miles from Wickersley. Marjorie always remembers it as having a strange atmosphere, almost as if the weight of its history was bearing down upon the place.

Blyth is very close to Torworth and Joe now turned his attention to that village where he and Mary Evelyne had first lived on getting married. Much of the land in the village was owned by Lord Galway and news eventually came to Joe that his lordship wished to sell thereby enabling Joe to acquire Manor Farm in Torworth with its 78 acres for £1100 and at the same time he bought other land in the area. Manor Farm was a working farm and Joe intended to continue its operation, his first move into the world of farming. The parishes of Ranskill and Torworth were in dire need of a recreation ground for the use of the local children and Joe proved his munificence by letting the parishes take 5 acres of his land at a nominal rent to provide the much needed recreational facilities. On part of his newly acquired land abutting the Great North Road he built a restaurant for his Greek friend, known as Vlacko, which still stands, a 1930s building, though much renovated, but it is no longer a restaurant and is now a private house. The restaurant custom in those days would have largely been from passing trade on the Great North Road but the building of the A1 bypass away from the village would have taken away all possibility of a viable eating-house in that situation, forcing the restaurant to close.

CHAPTER THIRTEEN:

WAS IT ALL BECAUSE OF THE BED?

The Bed

It is a huge bed, a half-tester of tremendous weight and it is not certain exactly when Joe initially set eyes on it but it is very possible that he saw it for the first time when Blyth Hall came on the market in 1929. The bed had been there for many years, the property of Lord Barnby and his family. Some have believed that it is a 16th century bed but a closer examination of it reveals that the workmanship is of a much later origin, and the story that it came to Blyth Hall from the Great Exhibition in the Crystal Palace in London in 1851 is much more likely. Joe's protracted transactions concerning the Nottinghamshire stately home included this bed and at some time during those negotiations he became the proud possessor of it. With his fascination for solid timber he valued it highly, so highly in fact that he was prepared to go to the greatest of lengths to take it home to Listerdale and use it. The trouble was, however, that the bed needed grand baronial surroundings to show it off to its best advantage and Joe's bungalow, although substantial, could in no way accommodate such a large item of furniture. Was it perhaps more than coincidence that he was at this point thinking of a spectacular extension to his bungalow at Listerdale?

Plans for this breathtaking extension were lodged by Joe with the local planning authority and are dated December 30th, 1929, which is conclusive evidence that he must have been considering it almost immediately after he had entered into negotiations that resulted in his purchase of Blyth Hall, and some months before the tragedy of Mary Evelyne's death. This was to be no ordinary 'add-on' to Joe's bungalow for when it was finished it was rightly christened 'The Castle'. It is built of dark brick-work of various patterns and bonds and stands solidly four-square, its castellated roof-line towering over Bawtry Road. The extension fits the original bungalow snugly and manages to create the impression that the bungalow is the extension rather than the other way round. In this castellated wing Joe created a large, high-ceilinged room on the first floor and in it stands the great bed to this day.

There was one more twist to the story of bringing the bed home to Listerdale. When the building was completed it was discovered that, although the bed could be dismantled, it was even then too large to enter the front door and be carried up the stairs to the bedroom, so there was no alternative but to demolish the newly-built outside wall and hoist the largest piece of furniture most people had ever seen up to first floor level, then pass it into the room through the hole in the wall, re-bricking the wall after the operation had been completed. The legend of 'Lister Castle' was born. The building works went on for a considerable time and many years later, in a feature article in the *South Yorkshire and Rotherham Advertiser* of 1st March, 1958, Joe's son, Clifford, recalled how for a long time he had to walk across a plank to get to his bedroom, the door of which was no more than a blanket hung over the opening.

Castle House before the road was widened.
The original bungalow can clearly
be seen on the left

Before Bawtry Road was widened the new building would have dominated the scene much more than it does today. Built on a slight rise from the road, there were sweeping lawns down to the old narrow thoroughfare and it is ironic, considering his vigorous campaign for road-widening, that when the dual carriageway was eventually built long after Joe's death, it was his garden which suffered the most. An aerial photograph taken of the building around the time of its completion clearly shows the narrow strip of land which Joe had sold to the Council some years before and which was earmarked for the widening of Bawtry Road. It is clear that he only thought of the widening of the single carriage road during his vigorous campaign but when it was decided in 1969, many years after his death, that the road needed to be up graded to a dual carriageway, the strip of land was not wide enough to accommodate the extra carriageway without encroaching on his garden and those of the neighbouring houses. Much of the Castle's garden was taken for eventual improvement of the road and traffic now thunders on the area where once his lawns had stood, while the splendid view of his property is now largely lost, trapped behind a high retaining wall which blots out much of the ground floor, leaving the upper windows and castellated roof visible from Bawtry Road. How Joe would have received the news that a proposed dual carriageway would take quite a bit more of his beloved estate will never be known but undoubtedly he would have approached the question with his usual combative style and fought for the interests of his creation.

The building of Joe's castle was completed by 1934 and it contains much that reveals Joe's eccentric character.

When he designed his daughter's bedroom he ordered that the leaded windows were not to be constructed in a straight fashion but should be made crooked. His explanation for this particular quirk, given with his own inimitable sense of humour, was that if she ever came in drunk the windows would then look straight. Hidden in the exterior brickwork are patterns of human figures which are another example of this extraordinary sense of humour while on one chimney stack there is Joe's monogram, JCL, and on another there are curious mouldings on the top at the four corners. They bear a striking resemblance to human backsides or, with only a bit of applied imagination, they could be taken for other parts of the male anatomy! They most certainly contain more meaning than simply an example of Joe's racy sense of humour and local tradition has it that they are an indication of Joe's opinion of the various local authorities with whom he had to deal. On the front of the house facing away from the road and overlooking the still extensive garden at the back is an enigmatic ancient Greek quotation which translates as *Fruits of the Dead Sea*. It is also repeated in Welsh on another outside wall. The Welsh is easily explained, being in deference to his Welsh sister-in-law, Megan who came to keep house for him after Mary Evelyne's death, but the quotation itself has puzzled many people. There is no clue in any of the papers left behind by Joe and it seems a somewhat bitter sentiment for a man of such optimistic frame of mind as Joe Lister most certainly was. The only connection he had with Greece was through his friend, Vlacko, the Torworth restaurateur, and that a tenuous one. Joe would certainly have mastered some ancient Greek at Rotherham Grammar School but why choose that particular quote? The Dead

Sea is renowned for the absence of marine life because of its salinity and its only 'fruit' is the salt.

'Fruits of the Dead Sea'
Note the crooked windows above

Joe was now in his late forties and it was at this point, as he was the building his castle, that he decided to adopt a coat-of-arms. It is to be seen in several of the windows of his new large house and consists of a mailed arm emerging from a cloud and holding aloft a sword. There is a motto in French, *Une seule me suffit* - 'But one is enough for me'. Joe has left no explanation as to why he chose this particular coat of arms and it only appears in the building and was never carried on his stationery. It was never registered as official and appears simply as decoration. There are, however, some clues as to its origin.

Coat of Arms

The motto is to be found in an ancient French book, *Devises et emblemes*, compiled in 1691 by Daniel de la Feuille who produced the document to record all the known emblems and mottoes of his time and in the original the device accompanying the motto consists of an arrow pointing at the Pole Star, which explains the feminine, *Une seule*, obviously referring to *Une étoile*, a star. On the same page of the document is the representation of an arm emerging from a cloud but it is not mailed and in this case is holding aloft a book. It can never be ascertained if Joe had seen a copy of de la Feuille's book in his search for a suitable emblem but the coincidence is remarkable. Another theory is that he based his idea on the Foljambe coat of arms which has as its crest an armoured leg, or *jambe*, the connection here being that Joe purchased some of the land that was included in Listerdale from the Foljambe Estate, in particular Dalton Magna Farm. De la Feuille's book may explain the origin of the use of the feminine in the motto but does not explain what Joe was thinking about when he chose that particular inscription. After he was made a widower at the age of 44, while he was in the process of building his castle, he never married again and was he therefore thinking of Mary Evelyne, his one and only wife? It will never be known but remains part of his enigmatic personality, part of that drive and imagination which led to the creation of Listerdale and his vision for the future of his estate.

Joe furnished his castle in keeping with his larger-than-life personality. The rooms in the castle block are large and lofty, panelled with oak grown in Thoresby Park in Nottinghamshire and the building contains a large teak staircase with a half-landing where there stands a suit of armour, known by younger members of the Lister family as 'The Iron Mester' and regarded by some of them as rather frightening. They may have been thinking of some of the thrillers they had perhaps seen in the cinema and no doubt they imagined that one day it would move its arm and grab them as they walked past it, scaring the life out of everybody. The origin of the staircase is unclear but it was certainly brought to the house complete from elsewhere. One story maintains that it came from a shop owned by Boots the Chemist and another holds that it came from a house in Sheffield called 'The Thatched House'. Photographs of it in its original setting give little clue but the large teak doors that lead off the hall and landing definitely came from a Boots' shop somewhere in the north-east of England because when they were dismantled for cleaning, Malcolm Leader, who was in charge of the operation, discovered the firm's details were clearly marked on one of them. The substantial ceiling beams were once owned by the Duke of Newcastle and came from the house which had existed in Clumber Park in the 'Dukeries', Nottinghamshire, as were the stone flags used for the ground floor. The large fireplace, decorated with heraldry, including Joe's own, was specially made for the house and adds to the 'baronial' appearance of the interior.

Joe's castle cannot fail to impress with its audacity and assertiveness and, whereas the aerial photograph taken just after it was built gives little clues as to its future setting, the rear gardens have been laid out boldly and have matured into fine sweeping lawns and terraces. There are garages which were built for his fleet of cars which became very much his pride and joy and now the neighbouring bungalow has been taken over as the Listerdale Estate Office. One end of Marcliff Crescent has been closed to vehicular traffic and the whole property is now seen to stand in extensive and attractive grounds. Joe, born in a small semi-detached house, now had his large property and could live as befits any minor landed gentry and at the same time he was able to keep a paternal eye on his estate. For that concern he is famous in the Rotherham area as he was no speculative builder who simply moved on after making a fortune to find opportunities for further speculation and further riches, showing no interest in his creation. Joe was an attentive landlord whose philanthropy became the stuff of legend in the locality. When Joe died in 1947, Castle House became the home of his son, Clifford, and his wife. In Clifford's notes, added to Joe's 1936 account, he records his own marriage to Joyce Stickland from London on August 7th, 1948, and adds his comments on the property:

> [Clifford and Joyce] set up home at Castle House, Listerdale,
> where they lived frugally for many years in a property which
> was far from comfortable and in many ways unfinished as Joe
> Lister had built his house in bits and pieces and never really
> finished any of it, due no doubt to having no wife to make a
> home for.

Whatever Clifford may have thought of his father's
house, and he did add a further note some time later
indicating that 'we now have a loved home and garden',
Joe's personality is still very much in evidence at Castle
House and a study of the building only serves to deepen
the mysteries surrounding that personality. Joe clearly
liked his little jokes and there is much humour in the
fabric but there are also many puzzles to be found and it
seems typical of the man that he can still keep us
guessing so many years after he died.

CHAPTER FOURTEEN:

DRIVING AHEAD

It was a cold January morning in Bridlington, a seaside resort on the north-east coast of Yorkshire, and the magistrates of the town had solemnly assembled at 'ten o'clock in the forenoon' to hear the cases for that day. There were the usual incidents of theft and petty larceny and it looked as if it would turn out to be an uneventful session until one defendant in particular appeared before the Bench. He was Joseph Charles Lister and he had been summoned to appear on a charge of driving an unlicensed vehicle. The prosecution alleged that the county taxation office had sent no fewer than four reminders pointing out that the vehicle needed a renewal of tax if it were to be kept on the road, and that all these reminders had been ignored, the current tax having by that time expired. Joe's only defence was that he never opened letters. He told the Bench that he had not opened a letter addressed to him since 14th December, 1935, more than a year before. 'If I saw all the correspondence and begging letters I get I would never get through. I have now resolved to open no more letters as long as I live', he informed the surprised Bench.

After due deliberation they decided to fine him ten shillings (50p) but he had one more surprise up his sleeve. Telling the Bench that he had seven cars, owned land in ten parishes and had about 800 tenants near Rotherham, he said that they might as well make the fine £1 as he was going to pay that anyway and they could then give ten shillings to the local hospital. After that the Bench really had no alternative but to offer their thanks to him for his understanding and generosity!

Joe was born before any of the roads in Britain saw their first motor car but motoring became one of his abiding passions and the first car owned by him was an early Clement-Talbot; but the one he used for his honeymoon after his marriage to Mary Evelyne was an unusual car, a Sabella, and a photograph in the family album shows Joe at the wheel of this car in 1914. It was an open two-seater. The tyres were of the solid variety and the belt drive can clearly be seen below the chassis and looped round the rear wheels. Its sole means of forward illumination was a single acetylene gas lamp mounted on a bar in front of the radiator. The honeymoon journey on solid tyres could not have been very comfortable for either the bride or the groom, and one of the most striking peculiarities of the car is the fact that it had 'tandem' seating with the driver sitting behind the passenger – the original 'back seat driver', possibly. It is hard to imagine how, if the passenger were tall, the driver could see the road ahead. Rear seat driving also meant that there was an extremely long air-pipe to the horn which was mounted near the front mudguard and operated from the rear one. Sabella cars, perhaps more accurately described as 'cycle-cars', were made between 1906 and 1914 in Camden Town, London, by Fritz Sabel who became quite well-known in the light car business. For a time, they became popular as family cars and despite their small size and light weight could easily accommodate a family of two adults and two children, but undoubtedly without much comfort. By driving a Sabella in 1914 Joe Lister certainly put himself in the category of 'new motorists'.

In June, 1926, Joe purchased a Model 70 Willys-Knight. This was an American car manufactured by the Willys-Overland Company of Toledo, Ohio. It was famous for the ultra-quiet running of its sleeve-valve engine, invented by Charles Knight of Chicago, Illinois. It obviously captivated Joe who wrote glowingly of it in a letter to the firm on October 20th of that year. He had had some trouble with the speedometer (he often had this trouble with his cars) and admitted that it might have something to do with his manner of driving, 'there's nothing like the violent acceleration and deceleration of a Willys Knight for chewing speedometers up'. He praised its ability to climb hills from a standing start in top gear and 'pick up speed all the way up'. He then continues with tongue in cheek whilst at the same time providing clear evidence of his obsession with the ownership of cars:

> If by any chance at a future date you should describe the Willys Knight as a "No Trouble Car" you may expect immediate repudiation from me as it has been a source of endless trouble since purchasing.
>
> In the first case I bought it for the Wife and I have endless trouble persuading her to lend it me instead of my own (she says that now quite a number of train journeys I used to make I find excuses for accomplishing by road, if the Willys Knight is available, otherwise, if my own car, the train has it) furthermore when the speedometer is working I am called upon to explain how if I have not been tearing round the landscape I have managed to do say 200 miles, transact business, have lunch and be home under seven hours (the beauty of a defunct speedometer is that it tells no tales).
>
> One consolation the Wife has is that the Willys Knight is going the right way to enable her to wear widows' weeds at an early date, for somewhere back in my ancestry was one a

Swineherd in Sherwood Forest and I am a throwback and the nearest I can get is being a Road Hog as whenever I come across a Car of whatever make that is removing the Moss from his Tyres I usually get in front to shew him how it is done as this is an operation in which the Willys Knight is second to none.

Having owned 61 Motors and covered over 400,000 miles I have no hesitation in stating that the Willys Knight Saloon I now have has given me the most satisfactory service of the lot as the damned thing starts up <u>every time</u> on the switch. I can find no excuse for using my Yankee Cuss words on it and up to date the back axle has not overtaken the front one, but one day it will and if shortly after that time one of your New Willys Knight Engines develops a sighing noise it will be that of the spirit of,

Yours truly,

J. C. Lister

The following day he wrote to the *Motor* magazine about the car claiming that he had done over 10,000 miles in it since its purchase in June. He had a few complaints such as his belief that the headlights were not ideal but 'as regards the running of the car and its ease of handling I can suggest no improvements as there are none necessary'.

It is not known exactly how many cars in total Joe Lister purchased in his lifetime but a letter written six years later, dated October 10th, 1932, gives a better idea of his motoring career. It also enables us to work out his average rate of mileage per year. The letter is addressed to the Alvis Car & Engineering Company Ltd. with whom he was to have considerable dealings. This company, founded by T. G. John in 1919 and which was based in Coventry, began manufacturing cars in 1920. The Willys-Knight had ceased production in 1932 which might explain why Joe in that year turned his attention to Alvis cars. Joe had just purchased an Alvis Speed 20 saloon a few months before he wrote the letter and he was not all that pleased with it. It must have been one of the early Speed 20s for they were only made from 1932 to 1936. Alvis had designed them for exceptional performance. On the day the letter was written he had taken it out with a friend as a passenger and driven over the Snake Pass in Derbyshire. At the top of the pass the car had a puncture when they were in the middle of a rainstorm! To his horror the jack supplied with the car would not fit under the rear axle. His letter continues:

> Your jack is the essence of inefficiency not having the necessary lift and impossible to work from the rear when used under the back axle and in consequence my friend and self have ruined two good macks and taken one and a quarter hours to do a job that should not have taken 5 minutes to do in fitting the spare wheel.
>
> Why do you people invariably spoil an otherwise good job by some oversight that the least consideration would remedy?
>
> I have had three cars at a time now for some years and when I purchased the Alvis it was my 72nd motor and since then I have bought an MG and shall be at the [motor] show next week to buy my 74th (having 16 Sunbeams, 16 Austins).
>
> Two years ago I passed my 750,000 miles of motoring so pride myself I know the difference between the radiator and the bonnet and as my motors have included cars without steering wheel, carburettor, magneto or sparking plug I know a legitimate grouse when I see it.
>
> Get the 'hopeless dawn' who turned this car out with the jack to have a cine taken of him jacking up from a <u>flat</u> tyre, with gallons of rain and buckets of mud available and a decent suit to wipe his hands on and have it distributed to your service agents to show incompetents like myself how our past motoring experiences have been wasted.

Joe and Marjorie with MG

He then goes on to list a few more of the defects he had discovered, including the wind screen wiper which was the second one to be fitted to the car and still only 'wipes everything but [the] part in front of the driver', the speedometer which 'lies like hell' and 'shows 100 when doing 93' and the Servo brakes, 'God help 'Em, no use at speeds above 40', and then gives a vivid illustration of his dare-devil motoring style:

> I came home from London a few days ago leaving 10-15 a.m. arriving here 12-57 p.m. 161 miles 163(sic) minutes and it is 80 miles from here to Bridlington which I do comfortably in one and a half hours or less if my passengers don't stop me to gather blackberries or mushrooms.
>
> In days gone by some of my old buses grew moss on the tyres while in motion, but I find your Juggernaut has a passion for leaving the rubber on the road instead of accumulating moss, but this is partly due to my advertising, as I almost invariably find some onlookers anxious to see the bus get into

motion, when I set too(sic) to drive off after stopping anywhere. "Sithee one o' them theer posh Alvis Cars" or similar remark from the spectators certainly calls for a spectacular get away with which I try to oblige them and as I have been laid out 11 times in Motor smashes it is far better to have a car that bumps efficiently rather than one that is only apologetic.

Joe must have touched speeds near or above 100 miles per hour many times to have completed the journey from London to Rotherham at an average speed of 60 miles per hour. It is true that the roads would be far less congested than today with almost a complete absence of traffic jams but it was also a time when there were no motorways and few bypasses or stretches of dual carriageway. Comparison of the two letters also reveals that between 1926 and 1930 Joe had driven over 300,000 miles! That is an average of over 75,000 miles each year. During that period he must have spent the greater part of his time at the wheel of a car 'tearing round the landscape' covering an average of 200 miles each day and it perhaps explains the mystery of what happened to his cars as some of them must have been run into the ground.

Clifford Lister recorded a story of one of his father's hare-brained trips to London in the 1930s, and his mischievous readiness to flout convention, when he took some friends to Rotherham station to catch the early morning train to London and Clifford came with him for the ride, although still in his pyjamas. At the station one of the friends remarked that it was a great shame he wasn't going with them so they could all have a day in London together. On the way home Joe suddenly decided that he would surprise them all by driving to London at breakneck speed and be at the station in

London to greet them. Clifford was still in pyjamas and there was no time to return home and get him dressed so the pair of them continued in the direction of the Great North Road, turned on to it and proceeded at speed to London where the surprised friends found him at the rail terminus. They spent the day together; but what about Clifford's attire? Joe solved this question by buying a coat for Clifford to wear over his pyjamas, completely ignoring all the stares that this attracted as they made their way around the capital. The whole party came home in Joe's car and they stopped for a meal on the way, dining well as Clifford records. Joe announced to the curious and startled diners in the restaurant that as it was late and Clifford needed to go to bed immediately they arrived home in Listerdale, it was fitting that he was already in his night attire.

The seventy-sixth car purchased by Joe was a 1932 MG Midget which he described as 'the lousiest bus' he had ever bought and he wrote an extremely angry letter to the Rotherham Motor Company who sold it to him. Dated 28th December, 1932, the letter begins:

> Being an upright, honest, sober and industrious man of full age I do not know just how to commence this letter, being yet filled with the peace on earth business, but to confine my remarks to language of extreme modesty. Just why in seven hells didn't you have me certified as insane instead of letting me buy that alleged car to wit 1 MG Midget (I won't say complete as the bloody thing has been coming through in penny numbers since I bought it)
>
> ....The sight of it now makes my nose bleed and all the good things I have said about it to my motoring pals has about put the tin hat on this new model (I was just wondering how many more you have sold since I first began broadcasting about mine).

He ends his letter by pointing out that he had already bought eight or nine Morris cars in his time but that this would be the last he would ever buy and demands that they take it back 'and sell [it] to some poor bloody fool for whatever you can get and use the proceeds as part payment for some other car that will run'. There is no record that this actually happened but there is an anecdote that he was driving an MG one day and gave a lift to a lady who admired it. It is said that Joe gave it to her as he did not like the car. She returned next day with the car to say that she could not accept it as Joe must have been drunk to have offered it to her. On being told that Joe was, in fact, a strict teetotaller but a bit eccentric, she was persuaded to accept it! Another story of an act of kindness by Joe in one of his motor cars has been provided by Patrick Burns who now lives in Singapore but was born in Bramley, near Rotherham. His grandfather, who worked as a steel turner in Masborough, knew Joe as they lived very close to one another on Bawtry Road. He used to cycle to the steelworks from Wickersley every day, a distance of over three miles, but on one occasion when he was cycling home he discovered that there was something wrong with his cycle, meaning a weary trudge home through the centre of Rotherham and up the hill to Listerdale. But Joe came to the rescue, stopping his sports car on the outskirts of Rotherham when he caught up with him and offering a lift home which was gratefully accepted.

The Stag Inn is a famous landmark at a crossroads on the route from Rotherham to Bawtry and in 1932 a new roundabout was built to control the traffic at this busy intersection following the construction of Valley Road as a bypass to relieve congestion in the town centre. It did not escape Joe's attention as this would be a route he would use often on his journeys to and from Rotherham. Addressing his remarks to the Editor of the *Rotherham Advertiser* he first asked 'who is responsible for the brainy lay out near the Stag Inn where the new £100,000 road crosses the old main road into Rotherham?' He did not think that the new road would be used in preference to the old main road as there were too many hills and then finally in his letter, dated November 4th, 1932, he homes in on his real target, the roundabout:

> If the cross roads had been left open and paved all over, anyone could have crossed in safety, but now it will be quite a work of art to pick the proper channel, unless the Council are going to employ the unemployed as pilots, but then it will be another work of art finding them in a fog.
> Yours
> J C Lister

There is a corollary to his letter: he was giving a lift to one of his tenants just after the roundabout was built and as they approached it he refused to use it, driving straight through the middle with the remark, 'I'm not going round that bloody thing.' Joe's nephew, Ian, relates how he believes that his uncle was charged with an offence over this incident and, characteristically, argued with the magistrates in Rotherham who threatened to fine him £5.00 for his truculence. He is said to have replied that he would pay £25.00 as £5.00 would not 'express his contempt for the court'.

Between 1932 and 1934 Joe bought fourteen more cars and the *Autocar* magazine in March of 1934 reported that he then owned a fleet of five cars, an Alvis Speed Twenty, a Lanchester 18, a Daimler 15, a Lanchester 10, and an Austin 12. Perhaps with tongue in cheek, the magazine continues: 'Apparently he was looking them over the other day, when he discovered that they are all saloons, so he has ordered a very special open Speed Twenty, which is costing him £1,300. Altogether he has owned eighty-six cars – at least, that was the number last week; by now the total may be ninety-six.' Joe had obviously been in touch with the magazine in his characteristic trenchant style for the article concludes with, 'Mr Lister does not brag about this; he only mentioned his cars to support a statement he made in a letter which, unfortunately, cannot be published without the whole lot of us appearing in the libel court.'

The publication of Joe's multi-car ownership evoked a critical response from a reader of the *Autocar* - Mr. Francis, who lived in Southgate, London. In a letter addressed to Joe dated 12th March, 1934, he takes him to task for possessing so many cars and then ordering another one for £1,300 on top of that. 'Do you not think', the letter reads, 'such actions, or statements thereof, would remain better unpublished? They create a very bad feeling among certain classes, and are of the order that turns a country extreme Socialist at one effort. Remember that the interest on that amount of money is keeping families of half or dozen or more.' Any reply which Joe made to this admonition has not survived but one can imagine his chuckle. It might even have been one of the letters that finally convinced him not to open any more addressed to him!

The specially built Alvis was duly completed and was the subject of an article in the *Motor* of 22nd May, 1934. It was not as it happens an open car but was described as 'a car of outstanding interest [which] has just been supplied to Joseph Charles Lister, Esq., of Listerdale, near Rotherham, by the Lancefield Coachworks, of Wrenfield Place, London, W.10...a fully streamlined four-door, six-light saloon on an Alvis Speed Twenty chassis, and is notable for a very graceful appearance coupled with an unusual amount of passenger and luggage accommodation.' The 'six-light' refers to the extra large rear quarter-light windows. The same article reported that it was Joe's '59th car' which was obviously a mistake as he himself had written in 1932 (see above) that he was then on his 72nd car.

Joe with his specially built Alvis Speed Twenty

The Alvis was considered of revolutionary design as the article continues:

> The treatment of the bonnet is interesting, for when the single-piece lid is lifted the built-in wing lockers, at both sides of the engine are exposed. These are insulated with asbestos and each contains a spare wheel and a tool box. The headlamps are recessed into the wing-fairing and the sidelamps are concealed in the curve of the wings. The windscreen is exceptionally wide, giving good vision. It is of the fixed type.
>
> There is nothing unwieldy about the car. It is well proportioned and gives the impression of having been built "in one piece". Certainly distinctive, there is nothing that makes it in any way freakish. Seeing it simply convinces that this type of body will come quite soon.

The car was one of Joe's prize possessions and an illustration of its design was sketched by Joe himself directly onto the wall at the Alvis factory, remaining there for many years until the wall was finally demolished. In 1990, the family tried to trace the car's whereabouts if it were still in existence but without success. Its registration number, AYH 577, located it as being registered in London in May, 1934, but without the chassis or engine numbers it was impossible to trace it any further.

Joe's passion for motoring and his position in the locality virtually guaranteed him his place as President of Rotherham and District Motor Club and he was known for being outspoken at its meetings. On one occasion he had refused to attend the Annual Dinner on the grounds that he had no dress shirt. The officers of the club, not to be outdone, sent him a 'blue union' shirt and he duly turned up wearing it complete with a coloured muffler, white waistcoat and tailed jacket. The *Rotherham*

Advertiser in November, 1935, carried a photograph of the Club's Annual Dinner and Joe is shown presenting a cup to Rotherham's well-known motor-cyclist of the time, 'Archie' Bingham, but on this occasion he is shown wearing white tie and tails.

One of Joe's spectacular crashes

Joe's motoring activities continued until the outbreak of war in September, 1939, when it became, like house building, very much curtailed by the demands of the war. Fuel was immediately rationed by the issue of petrol coupons, and at first there was a 'Basic Ration' for private motorists but in due course this was stopped entirely because of the great need of the war effort. Motor fuel was then only available for essential users and many cars were 'laid up' for the duration of the war. Joe, who was by now farming as well as running the

Listerdale Estate, would have qualified for the small amount of fuel that was allowed, but in no way would it have enabled him to continue motoring to the extent that he had been doing in the years leading up to the war. After the war ended in 1945, it was easier to obtain fuel but, sadly, Joe's health had deteriorated and he was never again able to embark on his motoring adventures.

PART FOUR: THE GENEROUS YEARS

CHAPTER FIFTEEN:

A GLIMPSE OF THE FUTURE

Nowadays, an increasing number of people have taken to shopping 'on-line', attracted by its convenience and the facility to obtain goods without the necessity of leaving home. Joe Lister had thought of a similar idea before, in the 1930s, even though the concept existed only in his imagination. In his 1936 account he wrote of his regrets that there were no shopping facilities on his estate and complained that the retail financial benefits arising from his development were going to shops in 'adjoining properties'. By this remark he must have meant the shops along the Bawtry Road at Wickersley and there can be no doubt that Joe's building operations must have affected the prosperity of local retailers most favourably. He elaborates further:

> If I had the funds available, and as still sufficient energy and interest left to look after the place, I would have liked to have turned the Listerdale Estate into a kind of self-supporting community. In this respect, I would suggest between Black Carr and Springfield Road, building a large store – of what might be termed a co-operative variety, every house without exception on the estate to be coupled up by telephone to the store – which could be used as an automatic telephone exchange, if so desired. The telephone wires would be used for relaying wireless programmes – after the manner of the direct service now used. My reason for having the telephone centralised is this:- today, when hawkers are not allowed to travel the streets shouting their wares, it does not matter how cheap or how perishable his goods, the public cannot be made aware of it in an effective manner quicker. My idea – that say at 10 o'clock every morning a lever is switched over and

every telephone wire becomes the wire for the receiving set and the announcer at the Stores informs all the clients what their specialities are for the day, what cheap lines and perishable goods they have to offer at low rates. After the announcement the tenants would each 'phone their orders into the Stores and the goods would be delivered on what might be termed 'batches of adjoining houses' not, as now – a lot of shop-keepers sending up and down the different houses in the same street.

The opening remarks with regard to energy and interest are uncharacteristic of Joe whose zeal and enthusiasm for his beloved Listerdale Estate seemed to know no bounds. It could have been that the weight of the financial responsibilities which he had to shoulder in order to build his estate were proving a heavy burden for him, and that would have been unsurprising. What he means by 'a co-operative variety' type of store he does not make clear although it could have been that he envisaged sharing the ownership of the retail outlet with the tenants but the whole scheme never went beyond Joe's fertile imagination and the Listerdale population continued shopping in Wickersley and at the shops which eventually developed at The Brecks.

Rent collectors have now largely become a thing of the past but Joe Lister was very much involved with collecting his own rents from his tenants. Later, he included his family in the operation and Marjorie, his daughter, well remembers her days walking round the estate to collect the rents. Calling on all his tenants on a regular basis brought Joe into contact with the lives of people who were often struggling to make ends meet in the 1930s. He particularly noticed how difficult life could be for women who had to stay in the house practically all day with no-one to speak to and in 1936 his mind went to work on ways in which he could alleviate this:

> I often think of such things as communal feeding, where the women folk could each take a hand in different departments, which could vary from day to day – according to how they felt and so on, that husbands and children could come home to communal feeds say mid-day and tea-time, and if the rest of the day was spent in home-life, the women folk would then have a change – which otherwise could not be available – providing them with something different to see and talk about outside their own immediate house.

Joe's thinking anticipated the canteens that emerged in the munitions factories of the Second World War, but in the next breath he realised that for him this was but a pipe-dream, like the building of an estate shop, and while clearly he did not have the resources available to carry out this scheme, it reveals his vision for his estate. His canteen would be 'coupled up with such things as communal laundries, child clinics, nursing, etc,' and he genuinely believed that his estate was compact enough and with sufficient open space for all these to have been possible. He felt deeply for the unfortunate lot of many of his tenants and his 1936 account concludes with a statement of his concern:

> To go round and see the unemployed – only just able to keep their heads above water by practising the strictest economy, whilst other people are in employment – but would be content to work a shorter week to allow the others a chance of employment – if things were going to be better all round in consequence, it is rather disappointing to think that in this world of plenty – owing to mal-distribution, on the one side there is plenty, on the other side what might almost be termed 'starvation'.

Many of Joe's first tenants were young married couples who were moving out of the centre of Rotherham into Joe's estate set near attractive countryside. There is a story in the family that Joe was approached by the local district nurse who was experiencing difficulties in obtaining a rented house in Rotherham to enable her to marry her fiancé. She arrived with a supporting note from the local doctor. Joe was able to help and is reported to have told her in his colourful way, 'I'm letting houses to all these young buggers who will soon be having babies so we'll need you here'. Whenever a new baby did arrive on the estate Joe would visit the proud parents, never leaving before pressing a silver coin into the infant's curled hand. Joe had the land available for a school and he donated an area on the brow near to the site of his original wooden hut for the West Riding County Council to build an infants' and junior school set in extensive playing fields. It remains in use and it still provides education for the young children of the area. Not surprisingly, there was a high birth rate in Listerdale as Joe had predicted to the district nurse and in those early days he realised the need for proper maternity facilities. He also had acquired some land on the other side of Bawtry Road from his Listerdale Estate which he did not use for building houses and donated this for the building of a maternity home for the estate. It still stands, but it is now used as a local authority nursing home for the victims of dementia, a sign of the demographic shift that has occurred since the creation of Listerdale. For some years there was a community hall at Listerdale which was converted from an old hut that had been used as a store-room when the houses were in the process of construction. The hall was run by the Listerdale Social and Garden Society and there was a grand 'Presentation and Opening' on December 7th, 1933, the ceremony carried out by Joe himself, followed by a concert of music, a comedian and even an 'Elocutionist'. The whole event was accompanied by Miss Edna Cook, L.R.A.M. and Mr J. Saunders. It became very much the centre of the community and was still in use in 2003 when, sadly, arsonists broke in and destroyed it. It has been very much missed by the older Listerdale tenants but there has been no rebuilding and the estate is now without a meeting place of its own. Among the other acts of generosity was the annual bonfire night which Joe provided for the estate and each year he would ceremonially light the bonfire.

As Joe progressed he did not forget his old school, Rotherham Grammar School, and promised to endow a scholarship. For this he purchased a property in the Borough of Rotherham which was known as Alma House and it provided an income which he donated to the school for the scholarship. At one point during the Second World War the Governors of the School tried to persuade him to sell the property and invest the proceeds in securities but he declined on the grounds that the property would be worth more after the end of the 1939-45 War. He was eventually proved right but after he died in 1947 the building was handed over to the school which later sold it and invested the proceeds.

It is clear from the evidence that Joe's creation of the Listerdale Estate meant much more to him than a convenient way to make a lot of money. He was never a philanthropist in the sense that Lord Shaftesbury and George Peabody were, wealthy men who built housing estates for the poor from the fortunes they already held. The Peabody Trust, one of London's oldest and largest housing associations, was founded in 1862 and now owns and manages nearly 20,000 properties over much of London. Joe had to make a profit out of his enterprise or he would have failed and faced bankruptcy. His estate, whatever the state of its completion, would in all probability have been taken over by the local council in that case, but he would have been ruined. Beyond the obvious profit motive there was a genuine desire to do what he could to improve the living conditions for many people during those inter-war years. Unlike the history of house prices since 1945, he was not, as he completed his houses, even sitting on a capital asset which was increasing in value at the time – in fact, almost as soon as he had completed his estate of rented houses and was still faced with the colossal charges on his borrowings, the value of houses began to fall and continued to do so until the outbreak of the Second World War. If we take the Retail Price Index as a yardstick, the decade before 1939 was a deflationary period for more than half the time. In the early 1930s there was mild inflation as prices increased by a total of around 10 per cent in the three years from 1930 to 1933. Prices remained stable for about a year but after that and throughout the rest of the decade, they began to fall. These conditions were never repeated throughout the remainder of the 20th century but £100 in 1933 became worth just over £114 in 1939 when the outbreak of war saw the commencement of the inflationary cycle which has never been reversed and meant that anyone who invested in property in 1945 at the cessation of hostilities has seen the value of that investment soar to unimaginable levels. Joe Lister saw virtually nothing of this increase in the value of his assets because of his untimely death in 1947. At the same time as prices were falling earnings were rising in the 1930s and by 1939 were nearly 10 per cent above their value nine years before – in real terms there was a general increase in prosperity. Joe's activities meant that more people in the Rotherham area could share in the fruits of that prosperity and move into living conditions which were in many cases far superior to their previous experience, often in cramped living space in the centre of Rotherham with several households sharing few facilities. It took all his skill and ingenuity to make Listerdale a successful venture and the worry and responsibility undoubtedly took an enormous toll on his health.

The Rotherham and District Boys' Welfare Club was founded in 1933, taking over the lease of school buildings belonging to the Church but which were no longer required, and the Minutes of a meeting which was held in Rotherham Town Hall on 13th February of that year to discuss the opening of the Club record Joe as being present and agreeing to contribute £30 per year to the running costs of the establishment. His generosity and good business sense no doubt played a part in his being appointed to the Finance and General Purposes Committee. Lord Milton, of nearby Wentworth Woodhouse, was elected Chairman and it was agreed that the Club 'should be open to all boys in the district between the ages of 14 and 18, either in work or unemployed; it should be non-sectarian, [and] should be for the improvement of the minds and bodies of all boys becoming members...' Lord Milton formed a good impression of Joe for in a letter written to Joe by the Club's Honorary Secretary, W. Milnes, and dated 2nd March, 1933, Joe is informed that at a meeting of the Club's Officers held that day, 'Lord Milton referred to you as "Joe Lister" and "a good sort", and stated that you had done well for us'.

There is no mention in the Minutes of the forthcoming visit of the Prince of Wales, the future King Edward VIII, but in fact he made his second visit to Rotherham in that year and showed his interest in the Boys' Club by including it in his itinerary (his earlier visit had been in 1923 when he opened a power station). Joe was presented to the Prince along with other dignitaries and it was remarked and pointed out to His Royal Highness that Joe had not fastened his bootlaces. The explanation was very simple. A doctor, he explained, had once told him he would die with his boots on and he was of the opinion that if he left his boots untied he would have time to kick them off should he ever feel that he was in mortal danger. The truth of the story is that the doctor in question was well aware of Joe's habit of driving recklessly and was simply foretelling that Joe would die in a road accident. This amused the future King who is also reported to have remarked on the quality of the suit Joe was wearing for the occasion. Legend had grown up, perhaps mischievously encouraged by none other than Joe himself, that he only possessed one suit as he always seemed to appear in the same one. The facts are slightly different. On one occasion when Joe was visiting a tailor in Savile Row in London he enquired after material for making up into a suit. He was shown a length which he liked and was told that it was a very exclusive piece, only one bolt of that particular cloth existed which was enough to make seven suits. Joe's suits were designed to have large internal pockets in order that he could carry great quantities of paper-work, and it was this which gave rise to the idea that he always carried his office around with him, complete with all the items necessary for an 'office on the move'. Joe informed the outfitter that it could not possibly be exclusive if seven suits could be made from it, immediately decided he would have to make this bolt of cloth uniquely exclusive to him, bought the entire supply and had a succession of suits made from it. When the Prince of Wales, the future Edward VIII, admired one of these suits on this particular visit to Rotherham Joe informed His Royal Highness that he would be very happy to send him a suit-length of cloth which he duly did and it is reported that he received a letter of thanks written in the Royal hand, although the letter has not survived among Joe's papers. By this act Joe had obviously made the suits no longer exclusive but remained content that he shared that privileged position only with the heir to the throne.

Joe's interest in the welfare of young people had earlier brought him into one of his famous conflicts with local authorities, this time with Rotherham Corporation. In 1929 The World Scout Jamboree was held in Birkenhead, Lancashire, and a party of about twenty Boy Scouts from the Orange Free State, then part of the British Empire in South Africa, was entertained in Rotherham after the Jamboree. They were accommodated with families in the town who all extended typical Yorkshire hospitality, and during the course of their visit they were invited to tea with the President of the Local Scouts' Association. It was suggested that the Corporation should provide a bus for them in order that they could all arrive together for the tea. Rotherham dignitaries obviously did not consider these visitors to be very important for the organisers were told that a free bus would be out of the question but were informed that a concessionary fare would be

South African Scouts with Marjorie and Clifford at the bungalow, 1929

allowed for the visiting Boy Scouts to attend the tea on that occasion. It was to amount to no more than a 25 per cent reduction in the normal bus fare and the Corporation then sent the organisers a bill for fifteen shillings (75p) for the hire of the coach. Joe Lister was incensed at the treatment of these overseas guests of the town and paid for an advertisement to be placed in the local paper. After outlining the situation he continued in a vein which was heavy with sarcasm, including his reference to the possible reason why the Romans decided to build their settlement on the opposite side of the River Don from the spot where the town of Rotherham eventually developed. He was giving full vent to his feelings by holding the Corporation up to ridicule:

What did our LOCAL REPRESENTATIVES, with £3,000 to spend to BOOST the OLD TOWN do?

Did they put a clean table cloth on and send out for a Tin of Salmon, 1lb. of SOUSE, half a pound of Polony and 6 pennorth of Tea Cakes and make our visitors generally WELCOME?

THEY DID NOT!

A request was put forward that a 'bus might be placed at their disposal, when an invitation to Tea from The President of the Local Scouts' Association was accepted, thus giving the lads a chance to travel in ONE 'bus, which had not been possible on other occasions.

The reply was that the only concession that could be made was to reduce the 'Bus Fare from 1/- return to 9d.

...An account for 15/- has been received from the Rotherham Corporation for this 'bus, which broke down owing to its indignation and tore about like a Crab without any Claws...

If the Parents of these lads knew what a sacrifice our Corporation was making by reducing fares from 1/- to 9d., would not their bosoms swell with pride for the Mother Country? And what a tale to tell Zulus, Basutos, Kaffirs, Mashonas, etc., and what a point for our Missionaries on the advantages of civilization and Christianity!

It must have been Rotherham's special terms two thousand years ago for the ferry across the Don that caused the Romans to build a fort at Templebro' to store their savings in...

As quite a number of local people have spent more than 15/- each entertaining the Scouts and as Rotherham Corporation cannot afford to loose(sic) 15/-, Subscriptions are now asked for to clear this 15/- debt, any surplus being sent to Bloemfontein towards the cost of The Orange Free State's visit to this country; beyond the 15/- no deduction whatever will be made from the subscriptions, which will be greatly appreciated by

J. C. LISTER
LISTERDALE

It would no doubt have been much cheaper to pay the Corporation 15/- than pay for this advert, but how can our Corporation be fully appreciated otherwise?

CHAPTER SIXTEEN:

THE FISHERMEN'S FRIEND AND THE FARMER

There was often fog in Bridlington Bay and it was a hazard to the fishermen of the town who relied on the fog warning signal that was operated by the Harbour Master when the local skippers could not see their way into port. Whenever the fog descended, the Master or whoever was on duty at the time had to leave his office carrying with him the portable fog-horn which he duly set up on the end of the pier and switched on. As the fog cleared he had to return to the pier-end and collect the instrument for safe storage in the Harbour Office. It worked but it was very cumbersome and inconvenient as an operation. It all became very different in the spring of 1933. Among Joe's papers is a receipt headed 'Bridlington Piers and Harbour', dated 13th May, 1933, complete with two penny stamps and franked with 'Harbour Master, Bridlington'. It is for just over £123 and written in pencil are the words, 'Presented to J. Lister for Payment of Fog Signal'. Joe had donated a permanent fog-signalling apparatus to be installed at the pier-end and which was connected to the Harbour Master's Office from where it could be operated without anyone needing to leave the office to set it up. It was a major boon to the fishing industry of the town.

In the 1930s few people ever thought of travelling abroad for holidays; the cheap package holidays abroad did not exist and the English seaside was the best that most people could manage. Bridlington had become

Joe's favourite place for holidays; with his speed of driving he reckoned he could be there in and hour and a half from Listerdale (most people thought it should take three hours in those days, which is perhaps something of an exaggeration). He had bought property in the town in Fort Terrace and he and his family enjoyed weekends in the resort on the Yorkshire coast. He never built an estate there but he was intensely interested in sailing and the sea.

Joe at the helm, shoelaces undone
His own way of preventing drowning?

That part of the coast is famous for a particular design of small vessel, the 'coble', pronounced and sometimes spelt as 'cobble', a fishing boat with an upswept bow and no keel, which was built locally, clearly resembling the design of the old Viking 'long-boat'. Such vessels must have been seen off those coasts, and in the rivers, before the Norman Conquest of 1066. The coble design has endured for a thousand years and one of its characteristics is its suitability for launching off the gently sloping but often stormy beaches of the Yorkshire coast. The upswept bow or 'deep forefoot' made it possible to launch 'head-on' to the surf and the absence of any keel enabled it to float in the shallow inshore waters. The boat was held up while at sea by very deep rudders which could be unshipped and then used as gangplanks when the boat was brought in and beached. Whenever Joe commissioned a new boat he always insisted that it be built to coble specifications as it was his wish to help and preserve the boat-building traditions of the area. In the family collection there is a photograph of Joe at the tiller of one of his boats, dressed in his suit with watch chain visible, a somewhat crumpled shirt and, inevitably, wearing a pair of shoes with the laces undone.

He seemed to embrace every opportunity to show his generosity. When the Bridlington Sea Scouts needed a new boat it was Joe Lister who paid £50 for the old Flamborough South Landing Lifeboat, the *Matthew Middlewood*, which had seen 32 years service, and gave it to them and when Flamborough itself needed a new lifeboat, again it was Joe who donated it. The Coxswain of the lifeboat was Dick Cowling and he became a something of a special friend for whom Joe had the highest regard.

**Dick Cowling, Coxswain of the
Flamborough Lifeboat**
(Reproduced by kind permission of Arthur Cowling)

In September, 1934, some of the fishermen who manned
the lifeboat in emergencies were invited to Rotherham
together with their wives for a weekend as the guests of
Joe Lister. He saw to it that they were entertained most
royally. The bill for their accommodation at the *Crown
Hotel* in Rotherham survives and shows that Joe paid

a total of just over £11 for one night's bed and breakfast and two luncheons for 19 'Lifeboat Men'; only two of them indulged in 'Early Morning Tea'. Among this party was Dick Cowling, the Flamborough Coxswain, who had often said that he and his wife needed a new kitchen in their cottage but could never see their way to afford it. This gave Joe an idea, and Dick and his wife made their way to Rotherham without the slightest inkling of what Joe was up to. He had managed to keep his plans secret from them even though there must have been much activity behind the scenes, for he had arranged for builders and fitters to turn up at the Cowling's cottage over the weekend while they were away and completely install the new modern kitchen for which Joe met the entire cost. Dick and his wife had no idea what had happened until they returned home at the end of their visit to Rotherham and Listerdale. Joe obviously felt at home with these Yorkshire fishermen and they deeply mourned his death in 1947.

It was customary for the Lifeboat Fund to hold a street collection in Bridlington in the middle of summer when the town was swarming with holiday-makers and day-trippers. The lifeboat would be on show complete and ready to go into action; the public would be invited on board and inspect it to appreciate the dangers that the lifeboat crew were sometimes called upon to endure. Volunteers would be on the promenade with buckets which they would rattle to attract donations from the general public. The annual street collection was an important source of revenue for the service which relied entirely on funds which it could raise from donations and legacies. The Lifeboat Fund was a very popular charity and expected to do well from the generosity of visitors to Bridlington but on one occasion when Joe was staying in the town, he turned up on the quay and asked how the collection was progressing only to be told that the cash flow into the collecting buckets was slow. Characteristically, he took matters into his own hands, telling the fund organisers to get the lifeboat crew to stand by and he would improve the situation. He was accompanied by his son, Clifford, and they boarded a pleasure boat which sailed out into the bay. When they had reached a point some little way out but still in full view of the promenade, Joe handed Clifford his watch and his wallet, promptly stood up and deliberately fell into the sea, fully clothed. 'Man overboard!' shouted Clifford and so did everyone else who was near. On cue, the lifeboat roared into action, powering its way out into the bay and picked up a very soaked and bedraggled Joe Lister. The street collection never looked back.

Joe's abundant generosity would indicate that, by the mid-1930s, he was beginning to feel that he was more prosperous. He still carried the burden of his borrowings which were to continue for the rest of his life, but, although he may not have known it at the time, his risky enterprise had secured his own prosperity and that of his family. Joe reached his 50th birthday on October 27th, 1935, and this milestone birthday was marked by a very special occasion held in the Listerdale Estate Hall which was attended by a great number of his friends and tenants. He was by now such a sufficiently well-known local character that the proceedings were covered in some length by the *Rotherham Advertiser* a few days later in its edition of November 2nd under the simple headline, 'Mr. J.C.Lister'.

Arthur Pickles, of Joe's solicitors, Oxley and Coward, proposed his health but the highlight of the evening was the presentation to Joe of a 'china cheese dish in the form of a Dutch cottage'. It came complete with a 'legal' deed for 'the conveyance of a detached dwelling house in China'. The 'deed' was 'executed by "Evan Knowshoo", Solicitor', and included the following 'grant':

This conveyance made the 27th day of October, one thousand nine hundred and thirty five between criticisers without limit and Admiras Ltd. (hereinafter called 'The Grantors') of the one part and Joseph Charles Lister, Of Listerdale, Wickersley, in the county of York and elsewhere, Esq. (hereinafter in this deed and universally and unfortunately referred to as 'the said Joe' of the other part).

Now this deed witnesseth that for the purpose of effectuating the said desire and in consideration of the respect and affection (and possibly sympathy) which the Grantors bear towards the said Joe the Grantors hereby grant and convey unto the said Joe All that detached dwelling house with the base or pediment thereto And also the paint and decoration thereon and the emptiness thereon And together with the effluvia hereafter to be associated therewith and all the mites and maggots and other things that may creep, crawl, leap, jump and otherwise besport themselves in, under, over or upon the contents of the said dwelling To hold the said premises (if and so far only as the same may be held with being chained down) unto the said Joe to the Intent...

...That the said Joe may live many moons and enjoy many more of the said anniversaries as aforesaid even unto the day whereon the whiskers upon the chin of the said Joe may extend to the knees thereof.

The 'deed' ended with a series of declarations, including:

That notwithstanding that the pedal extremities of the said Joe are accommodated in footwear the laces whereof are not tethered...

Authorship of the document is unknown but Mr Pickles
of Oxley and Coward, Solicitors, must be the chief
suspect. The evening's celebrations included a supper
and ended with a programme of music, with Miss Edna
Cook, L.R.A.M. acting as the accompanist.

Joe had finished all his large-scale building operations
by the time of his fiftieth birthday celebration and from
then on turned his attentions to his farming interests.
He had purchased some farms close to his estate in the
1920s and used portions of the land for building and he
had bought Manor Farm in Torworth at Lord Galway's
sale. In 1929 he had entered protracted negotiations to
purchase Lindrick Hill Farm at Shireoaks, some
distance from Rotherham. Letters concerning this
transaction survive among Joe's papers but this farm is
never referred to in any of the lists of his assets that Joe
left behind. It does, however, appear in a very
comprehensive list of his 'Properties and Incumbrances
(sic) and showing Development' which was drawn up by
his solicitors, Oxley and Coward, in 1934. This
document also reveals that in 1934 Joe's debts had risen
dramatically from the £40,000 he owed in 1931 and that
he now was indebted to a staggering total of over
£243,000 in mortgages advanced to him for his
purchases of land and the subsequent development of
Listerdale (equivalent to over £10.5m. at 2002 values);
nearly £200,000 of this sum is represented by his
borrowings to build the 650 houses which formed the
Listerdale rented estate. This was a colossal burden
for an individual in 1934, taking up the greater part

of the income received from rents and subsidies simply to service the debt. These rents and subsidies were controlled and fixed but the interest rate on the borrowings, mainly from various building societies such as the Leeds, the Principality and the Halifax, was by no means fixed; it is small wonder then that he transferred some of his debt from time to time in order to obtain the most advantageous terms. Guarantees were provided by Rotherham Rural District Council but this was simply to protect the tenants, not Joe Lister, and should he default then the Council would have taken over the properties which would have become local authority housing. Joe would then have been declared bankrupt and would have lost his estate. Seemingly undaunted by this burden, he went on to purchase Moat Farm at Wickersley in 1935, an ancient site with some archaeological interest attached to it. In total, Joe purchased six farms, using some of the land on those nearest to his home for building purposes. Others were tenanted but Manor Farm, Torworth, and Moat Farm, Wickersley, were worked by Joe himself with the help of managers. Farming was not very prosperous during the 1930s as Britain was able to import a great deal of its necessary foodstuffs cheaper than it could be produced at home. Neville Chamberlain, the Prime Minister at the time, angered the farming community with a speech at Kettering, Northamptonshire, is which he virtually told them they were no longer needed. It took the outbreak of war in 1939, and the consequent difficulties in shipping foodstuffs from abroad, to bring British farming back into real viability and for the whole nation to be exhorted to 'Dig for Victory'. Joe became a familiar figure at the meetings of the local branches of the National Farmers Union where he was often in the forefront of the opposition to the increasing amount of form filling which the wartime Government demanded of farmers. He became so irritated by what he saw as this waste of time that at one point he staged what amounted to a one-man strike against the Ministry of Agriculture.

Bringing home the harvest with Joe as tractor driver. Marjorie is on the left

Joe's relationship with his tenants was usually very good but it was his interest in agriculture that led to a considerable difference of opinion on one occasion. A leaflet produced by Joe, dated January 26th, 1940, and headed 'TO THE RESIDENTS OF LISTERDALE' informed his tenants of a scheme he was proposing for the growing of potatoes and appealed for their co-operation in helping to 'produce some of the food they consume'. It was his intention to use one of his fields adjoining the Maternity Home near to the estate and grow main crop potatoes in '225 rows of minimum length of 150 yards'. He offered to be responsible for the cultivation but invited his tenants to take one row each and be responsible for the planting of the '450 to 500 (approx.) [of the] potatoes required'. When the potatoes were ready for harvesting the tenants would be able to pick them from their particular row and gather them in bags, but Joe would undertake the delivery. For all this the tenants were to pay ten shillings on joining the scheme and a further seven shillings and sixpence before gathering, 'so for seventeen shillings and sixpence and the slight labour of setting and picking, they would have the whole of the crop from a row at least 150 yards in length'. Joe anticipated a big demand and suggested that, as he had over 700 families on his estate and only 225 rows available, they should perhaps get together and share rows. He also expected to be able to donate money to The Red Cross Fund and Rotherham Hospital from the proceeds and suggested a competition for the heaviest yielding row.

Unfortunately, there were so few tenants ready to take up the scheme that Joe quickly decided to abandon it. Perhaps it was the money that was required to be put up by each family or the necessary work involved that put them off, but whatever the cause Joe did not mince any of his words in the next leaflet he put out on February 15th in which he berated the people of Listerdale for apathy towards his scheme. After describing the support he received as 'A DISMAL FAILURE', he continues:

> Just WHO is really expected to do ANYTHING in this
> crisis? Apparently the idea is to leave it to somebody else, but
> who that somebody is doesn't really matter so long as it isn't

oneself, anyhow, we all feel indignant that our enemies delight in saying that the British are fast becoming a degenerate race and no longer deserving of the proud position they have so long held in the World's affairs and it is their effort to usurp that position that is the chief cause of the present War, but what are we doing to prove there is no truth in their assertions?...

If you are incapable of assisting with your own food supplies, just who do you expect will help save your home when there is not a sound roof or window in this district after an air raid. Will it be THE SOLDIER, SAILOR or FOOD PRODUCER? who are already doing their best for their country.

Listerdale Estates is no longer involved in farming and the farms were sold after Joe had died. There is, however, some evidence that he hoped the family would continue the interest in farming. It is contained in a letter dated November 16th, 1945, and sets out some of Joe's wishes for the future. His first granddaughter, Gilian, was born in January, 1943, and the letter concerns her third birthday present. He was trying to buy '3 new young 4/5 months old Jersey Heifers that would be growing up alongside her and by presenting her with a further calf each year she would have a nice little pedigree herd by the time she was old enough to appreciate it'. He makes reference to his health now that he has reached 60 years 'and during my lifetime have sustained some rather good motor smashes which are now making up for lost time by taking their revenge out of me'. He admits that he does not know 'which are the best strains in the breed but would prefer a good butter fat yield to extra gallonage' He argues his case for not paying too much for them:

The Inland Revenue people have <u>flattered</u> me most highly by the amount of Income Tax they are expecting from me and as I expect they will insist on their demands being fulfilled I regret that for the time being I don't wish my present to wander far from the region of £200 cost, my income being <u>solely</u> derived from property and consequently paying more than its due share of war time costs.

If my idea of value for money is too silly to laugh at don't bother any further than beyond sending me a P.Card telling me to 'Go to ****', being a Yorkshireman (and proud of it) I shall not be in the least offended as I am not seeking 'Summat for nowt'.

He ends this letter by requesting that any reply should be sent to Moat Farm, Wickersley, Nr. Rotherham, rather than to his house at Listerdale as he is 'The man who never opens his letters'.

Joe's veiled prophesy about his life came true just over a year later when he died in January, 1947, and no-one in the family can remember anything of the heifer calves, which, if they were ever bought, presumably went in with the sale of Moat Farm just after Joe's death.

CHAPTER SEVENTEEN:

EPILOGUE

When the war commenced in September, 1939, Joe's building days were over. He had completed his property development as far as he was able and although he may have retained visions of what more could have been accomplished, it was not to be. He ran the estate throughout the war and continued with his farming interests which were of vital importance at the time as enemy action increasingly inhibited Britain's ability to import foodstuffs. His trips to Bridlington were curtailed but as a farmer he would have received a ration of petrol to enable him to carry on business – he needed transport to visit his various farms and supervise operations - but he never showed the old enthusiasm as, from 1940, his health began to deteriorate. It may have been, as he often claimed, that the high incidence of motor smashes in which he was involved were taking their toll. It must also be remembered that he was rejected for national service in 1914 because of kidney trouble and this was a weakness that remained with him throughout his life. In November, 1941, he produced his final account of his life. He was ill in Rotherham Hospital at the time and apologises for the sometimes 'disconnected' account as it was 'being written while nurses, friends, relatives, etc. are continually popping in and out'. As before, the statement is signed by Joe on every page but this time there are no witnesses as in the October 1930 document. It begins with a list of his properties which stretches to over two sides of foolscap paper; even then he admits that he might have overlooked some items, so large was his estate – he was receiving Exchequer subsidy on 598 houses but he had, however, to pay the local rates on these dwellings as the rents paid by the tenants were still deemed to include the rates. With all his experience of the housing market it is not surprising that he was able to predict the future reasonably accurately:

> Owing to the present War and probable damage to property by enemy action, it is very difficult to plan for the future as regards finances, although in one respect modern property will become more difficult to obtain and will cost considerably more to build for a number of years, thereby making the value of my houses considerably higher than at the time of building...
>
> Unfortunately, Bankers and Financiers owing to the system in operation in this country have a finger in far more pies than their actual so-called help justifies, resulting in more power coming into their hands instead of the actual producer and it is this that I consider the cause of the world's conflicts of later years. Up to a point, Banks have their uses but are primarily out to make money and are rapidly becoming such huge concerns that any local consideration that existed when Banks were not so grouped up has practically gone and the main consideration of headquarters is amount of turnover and security irrespective of whether the money required is for necessities or luxuries.

Despite this side-swipe at the money providers, his generosity appears to have been undimmed by any problems with his health. Quite often servicemen on leave would be accommodated and entertained at his home. Marjorie remembers that on one occasion she came home to discover two French Canadian servicemen staying at Castle House. Joe had apparently met them at Rotherham Railway Station and they had informed him that they had boarded the train intending to alight at the first sizeable town they came to and that happened to be Rotherham. They were on leave but had nowhere to go so they were invited home and stayed there for some time. Marjorie also remembers that this was all very well but food was rationed at the time and there was no extra to feed these young French Canadians who had enormous appetites. Somehow, they all managed. Joe had always shown great interest in the welfare of young people as his involvement with the Rotherham Boys' Club and the Bridlington Sea Scouts will testify and there is one story in circulation which illustrates so well his impulsive generosity, even in small matters. Joe once marched into a local stationery shop at the head of about half a dozen children none of whom were known to him. When they left the shop they all had new pencils and notebooks, courtesy of Joe Lister who had paid for them all.

Listerdale tenants had long had access to the land behind the estate which was a notable beauty spot consisting of woods, plantations and natural bathing pools. Joe's relationship with Rotherham Rural District Council had often been a stormy one but he undoubtedly recognised that without the co-operation of the Council, Listerdale would never have come to fruition. One of Joe's last gestures of generosity, in March, 1945, was a decision to open up this area to the general public and he offered the Council 122 acres of his land for an open space or public park. This offer was widely reported in the local press, the *South Yorkshire Times and Express* informing its readers that 'In its natural state the land is ideal for a park and has steep slopes and shady bowers. It is not estimated that a very large sum would be needed to convert the land into a public park'. On the same day, March 10th, the *Rotherham Advertiser* carried the story and even broke into verse in honour of Joe Lister. The piece of doggerel was written by an unknown versifier simply called 'The Squid':

Affection has no handles, so
We never call him Mister,
But always speak of him as Joe
When we refer to Lister.

Now he has given further cause
That we should go on liking
This worthy man with bearded jaws
And other points as striking.

For Joe has given us a park
A gift that's truly sporting
Where we may wander after dark
And do a bit of courting.

'Twill be a place for Cupid's darts
And tenderest embraces;
With bonds of love he'll tie our hearts,
Yet will not tie his laces.

The Rural District Council decided on a sub-committee to discuss the best means of developing the land but all its deliberations were to prove in vain. The costs involved proved greater than expected, Joe died early in 1947 before the gift was completely made over to the Council and the public park never came into existence. Had it done so there would have been a problem with access to the area for the roads to it were narrow and, although in 1945 most people would have approached it on foot or by bicycle, eventually the roads would need to be widened and car parks built to accommodate visitors. The land remains part of the Listerdale Estates and the Rural Council is no more anyway, having been swept away by the reforms to local government in 1974.

The year of 1945 was a time of great rejoicing for Britain for it saw the end of the huge conflict of the Second World War. Joe reached his 60th birthday in October, 1945, but there is no record of any form of celebration like the one that marked his 50th. Private motoring was allowed again even though petrol was still rationed and Joe could, if he wished, visit his beloved Bridlington but he was in fact not well enough to take a very active part in life or the administration of the estate. It was effectively being run by his Estate Foreman, Fred Harrison, a very skilled woodworker in whom Joe had placed a great deal of trust over many years, and the solicitors, Oxley and Coward of Rotherham were also very much involved in the administration of his affairs. Clifford Lister complained that he and Marjorie knew little of what was going on and regretted that, after Joe's death, they were so reliant on Harrison. The period of 1939-1945 had been a time of punitive taxation to pay for the war effort and Joe, as a property owner, had been hit extra hard, so hard, in fact, that he was forced to negotiate a suspension of the interest payments on his debts during those war years. Repairs to property had been extremely difficult during that period as well, and the houses that made up the Listerdale Estate, many of them as much as fifteen years old in 1945, were in dire need of maintenance, the bill for which was going to be prohibitively large. The future looked even more difficult and this added worry must have taken further toll of Joe's health. If he needed solace and escape he found it at Moat Farm which was a favourite place and in the few trips he could make to Bridlington. Clifford also records that his father never lost his generous habits and continued to lend his farm machinery to those farmers who were less wealthy than he was.

The early months of 1947 saw severe wintry conditions in Britain which did not help Joe whose health had been deteriorating even more so throughout the previous year. Earlier on, he had been diagnosed as suffering from cancer and had found life very difficult and painful, finally being forced to take to his bed in Castle House where he eventually needed constant nursing. He finally lapsed into unconsciousness and died in the evening of Monday, January 27th, 1947. The funeral was held on the following Thursday, January 30th, in St. Alban's Church, Wickersley, with the Rector, the Reverend Selby Johnson, officiating. The church was extremely full with people whose lives Joe had touched in his extraordinary career. All the family were present as were many of the tenants of the Listerdale Estate, but Joe's life had reached out well beyond the immediate locality and notable among the mourners were several from Bridlington including the Coxswain of the Flamborough Lifeboat, Dick Cowling and his wife, who both had so many reasons for mourning the death of their great friend. The Rotherham Rural District Council, with whom Joe had experienced such stormy relations at times, was represented by the Chairman and some of its members together with the Clerk to the Council. The many business firms with whom Joe had dealings throughout his career were also well represented as were the numerous charities and organisations which he had supported, including the Rotherham and District Motor Club. Among the many floral tributes to be seen in the church was one from Lord Fitzwilliam, the former Lord Milton whom Joe had met when the Rotherham Boys' Welfare Club was being set up in 1933.

Joe was not a member of any Church and by no means religious but in his address before the interment in Wickersley Churchyard the Rector of St. Alban's paid him an enormous tribute, beginning with a text taken from St. Matthew's Gospel (xxv, 40):

'Verily I say unto you, inasmuch as ye have done it to the least of these My brethren, ye have done it to Me'

In these words of our Blessed Lord we find our justification for paying Christian tribute to one who was not by profession of faith a zealous Churchman, but whose warm heart and ready hand endeared him to the poor and afflicted. Many will have cause to miss the generosity of this great hearted man. To those of us whose lip-service to the Master rarely translates itself into action these words should indeed provide a timely warning.

Joseph Lister was essentially an individualist, coming straight from the pages of Elizabethan history. He chafed under the petty restrictions and limitations of this age and needed wider fields for his striking personality. In his building, he built with originality; in his farming, the traditional methods were challenged at every stage. Here was man with a real gusto for life, who might well have taken for himself the motto: 'I count nothing outside of my province which pertains to humanity'. It was this unbounded interest in life which linked him to all activities in this village and district, which made him a friend of the Boy Scouts and Sea Scouts of the County and the benefactor of the Boys' Club in Rotherham, which endeared him to the fishermen of Bridlington and Flamborough, which made him our friend.

At the same time as Joe wrote out his last account of his life in November, 1941, he had made his last will and testament. It is written in his own hand, dated November 24th, 1941, and is extremely short. In it he bequeaths 'all my real and personal estate of any description' to be shared equally between his children,

Marjorie and Clifford. He makes it very clear that he does not wish the estate be sold but that 'EVERY effort be made to carry on with the estate as I should have done had I still been alive until such time as the mortgages on the property have been cleared off or considerably reduced'. After that he concedes that if either of his children wished to dispose of all or part of the inheritance 'every help and opportunity shall be given to the other to purchase that half so that the estate will remain as long as ever possible in one lot and under control of one of my family'. In total the will runs to no more than ten lines and is witnessed by two members of the staff of Rotherham General Hospital in which Joe was at the time lying ill.

Thus did the ownership of Listerdale Estate pass into the hands of Joe's children, Marjorie and Clifford; it is still run by the family today. It was a mixed inheritance when Joe died, consisting as it did of large assets in real estate carrying a tremendous potential for capital growth, which became apparent in later years when property values began their rise in the post-war period, but it also came encumbered with a frightening burden of debt at the time. The total value of Joe's estate was proved at £264,864 for probate purposes but it also carried a heavy liability for death duties of £43,000, approximately one sixth of all that he had owned when he died. There was no liquid cash available to meet this sum and assets had to be disposed of in order to pay the tax bill, beginning with some of the farms. In Clifford's account he lists the action that was taken and hints at the difficulties of those early years immediately after Joe's death:

> Moat Farm was sold to our solicitor, Frank Ogley (a bad move), Dalton Magna Farm was sold to the tenant, Mr. Burden, Dalton Parva Farm was sold to the tenant, Mr. Clegg, the flat and boarding houses at Bridlington were sold and the Hall and gardens of Blyth Hall, 7 acres of the field including the cricket pitch and the four cottages at the entrance being retained. A bank overdraft was negotiated and we entered a long period of frozen rents being ploughed into paying off the many debts which also included the building societies who were owed many thousands of pounds.

All this was on the advice of Fred Harrison and at that point neither Clifford nor Marjorie had anyone else to turn to. The great disadvantage for both of them was that throughout his extraordinary career Joe had always played his cards close to his chest, neglecting to keep them informed of his business activities during his lifetime and now, after his death, they were faced with the running of one of the largest private estates in the country consisting of 650 houses, having had no real training whatsoever in the management skills required for the maintenance of its viability. Many of the houses were reported to be in a poor state of repair in 1945 as maintenance had been extremely difficult during the war years. Harrison's advice was obviously to sell other assets beside the houses themselves in an attempt to keep the estate intact, as Joe had wished. This policy was pursued until 1971 when some of the houses began to be sold to the tenants and Clifford Lister obviously regretted waiting for so long before this course of action was taken when he wrote his account some years later in January, 1979:

Due to the influence of Fred Harrison we continued to live as though we were poor for longer than was necessary. It was not until we started to sell houses [on The Brow] that we had any spare cash at all. The prediction that my father made in his early struggle eventually came true and the estate which is left even after the disposals is today worth a few million pounds. The bulk of this is still owned by his offspring but for how much longer this can remain in the family only time will tell.

It was at that point, 1979, that it was possible to report that the estate was free of all encumbrances as all the building society loans and private mortgagees were paid off over the years. Post-war inflation had helped as it led to a greater rental income and large increases in the value of the estate's assets. In 1985 Clifford Lister reported that sales of houses had ceased. There are now 450 houses owned by Listerdale Estates which are rented out to tenants; the woods, valleys and streams to the rear of the estate are still open land for the use of the tenants. Joe Lister's legacy has survived and he has now become a legendary figure whose achievements in his comparatively short life are commemorated in the estate which bears his name.

The world will never be short of entrepreneurs, people who are prepared to risk everything on an idea, a vision, an opportunity but Joe Lister will remain unique. Residential estates will continue to develop but it is highly unlikely that a single individual, beginning with few resources of his own, will be able to build single-handedly a development of such magnitude as Listerdale. That is now the province of property and construction companies as the financial implications alone have become astronomical. The story of Listerdale's development is a fragment of English social history from the inter-war years and this portrait of its creator is meant to demonstrate how one remarkable man in his day seized the moment, often just in the nick of time, and by risking everything and more on a bold venture produced a positive result which still benefits many – a truly acceptable face of capitalism.

APPENDIX:

'HOMES FIT FOR HEROES'

At 11 am on November 11th, 1918, the guns fell silent, the slaughter ceased, the flames of destruction were extinguished and the lights of Europe began to come on again. Life gradually returned to normal and it slowly dawned on everyone's consciousness that in the four years of conflict and upheaval the world order had become different. It was not just that much of Europe needed reconstruction but fundamental changes had taken place in the way countries were to be governed. In 1918 Britain, women had been granted limited rights to vote in parliamentary elections for the first time; abroad, two old empires, the Austro-Hungarian and the Ottoman Empires, had vanished, but of greater significance perhaps for the future direction of Europe in the 20th century was the Bolshevik Revolution of 1917 which had installed a Communist Government in Russia. The significance of this revolution was not lost on the British establishment who quickly realised that measures had to be taken to stave off any threat of a similar revolution at home.

The men returning to their homes in Britain after four years of dreadful carnage expected a better life than the pre-war existence that millions had experienced. The 1914-18 war was the first 'total war', involving the whole population, not just the military profession, and this produced a significant change in attitude. Having been forced to fight for King and Country after the introduction of conscription in 1916, men came home with aspirations of an improvement in standards of living for themselves and their families and they looked to the Government to help them find it. Not surprisingly, many felt that a nation that had demanded their sacrifice owed them something in return, and the old notions of uncomplaining deference to a ruling class were beginning to crumble. In particular, the survivors of the horrors of the trenches looked for decent, affordable housing in which to bring up their children. This was in short supply as the census returns for the period reveal; building had simply not kept pace with demand. Even though there had been a great deal of house building in the last quarter of the 19th century, between 1911 and 1921 a total of only 300,000 houses had been built whilst the population had increased during this time by 1.8 million. More importantly, the number of 'potential households', which included those who normally would be living in their own houses but who were forced to share with others, increased by 1.1 million in the decade.

The first thing the Government had to do at the cessation of hostilities was to call a general election as the previous one had been held eight years before in 1910. The country went to the polls on December 14th, 1918, and this was an election very different from any that had been held before. All property qualifications for the franchise had been abolished and every adult male (over 21 years of age) was entitled to vote, provided they had registered, but the major departure from the old rules applied to women who were finally allowed the vote, provided they were over 30; they had to wait another ten years before they obtained the vote on the same terms as men. There was a low turn-out of only 57.2 per cent (many of the newly-enfranchised voters were still serving away from home) and the result of the election was a victory for the Lloyd George Coalition but it was to be dependent on Conservative support. The 'old' Liberals under Asquith were roundly defeated.

The Government knew that the men returning from the front were met with an appalling housing crisis which could fuel unrest and it took fright when it contemplated what had just happened in Russia. If David Lloyd George and his Coalition Cabinet, which contained many Conservatives, were not seen to take adequate measures to deal with this enormous social problem, no-one could predict how serious the outcome might be. Socialist revolution was very much in the air in post-war Europe. Despite the debate on 'the condition of England' question, governments prior to 1914 were not very concerned with social problems. They were only slowly coming round to the view that their intervention could directly improve the lives of the British people and what we now so naturally call the welfare state was then only just beginning; state pensions and national insurance (the forerunner of the NHS) had begun with David Lloyd George when he was Chancellor of the Exchequer in the pre-war Liberal Government.

Housing in the 19th century had largely been left to unregulated private enterprise, which built speculatively, and to charitable foundations whose interest had been the housing of the poor. The Victorian period spawned an impressive crop of philanthropists such as Lord Shaftesbury and Octavia Hill who had been a leading pioneer of philanthropy in housing up to her death in 1912 and central to her philosophy was the relationship between landlord, or landlord's agent, and tenant, a relationship which she attempted to 'humanise'. Her firm belief was that it was possible to build houses, rent them to the poor, be concerned with their welfare and still make a profit. She had little faith in the ability of massive state undertakings to alleviate poverty *en bloc* but believed that the condition of the poor could be elevated over time by enlightened individuals working for the benefit of other, less fortunate, people. Small-scale operations carried out at grass-roots level she considered were far better than large-scale and impersonal schemes and, had she lived to see it, she would undoubtedly have been encouraged by the work of Joe Lister at Listerdale whose building activities and close involvement with his tenants she would have admired. Although there are no references to Octavia Hill in the surviving papers of Joe Lister, in many ways he became the epitome of the 'Octavian' landlord. Joe Lister's own ideas turned out to be almost identical to hers.

The curse of 19th century housing had been the speculative high density building in the close neighbourhoods of the new 'factories' produced by the Industrial Revolution, particularly the insanitary 'back-to-back' dwellings, and although there had been a Town Planning Act in 1909 which had the effect of banning the construction of any more back-to-back dwellings, many still existed well into the 20th century and even beyond. Prior to 1909 all Acts of Parliament which had affected housing provision had their origin in the Public Health Act of 1875, a piece of legislation enacted by the Government of Benjamin Disraeli. This Act set up sanitary boards in local areas, the forerunners of the Rural and Urban District Councils which existed until local government re-organisation in 1974, and gave them the authority to enact bye-laws for the regulation of sanitary housing. The results can still be seen in our towns and cities where there are often rows upon rows of identical 'bye-law' housing set out in terraces lining perfectly straight roads laid out in a grid pattern. They were usually built to a high density of about 40 houses to the acre and those which bear date stones reveal how much building activity took place between 1875 and 1900. Although many terraces, particularly in London, have been 'gentrified' and made into 'bijou' residences, a great deal of them still have a characterless, boring and dreary aspect but it must be remembered that they were a tremendous improvement on what went before in the largely unregulated market for speculative builders. To be strictly fair, the bye-laws did not require the streets to be straight, merely that they conform to a certain width – it simply proved to be more economical to build in straight lines. Neither did the bye-laws insist that the houses should be identical, merely that they should have adequate ventilation, be built to solid specifications and also they were expected to be reasonably fire-resistant. Many families who moved into these houses when they were newly built must have thought that they had achieved a major improvement in their standards of living. One notable exception among builders had been 'Old Joe' Lister who, as we have seen in Chapter One, had built better than average housing and, as he intended his houses to be for sale, his streets never did present quite the same dreary aspect as much of the 'bye-law' housing in other parts of the country.

The newly re-elected coalition government of David Lloyd George attempted to meet the problem with its 'Homes fit for Heroes' policy, a slogan which had helped it win the election. It had set up a Ministry of Reconstruction as the war was ending in 1918 and had given it the task of assessing the nation's housing requirements. This Ministry quickly produced a pamphlet in which it stated that there was an acute shortage of between 300,000 and 400,000 houses in England and Wales, without taking any account of the need for slum-clearance. It became obvious that private initiatives alone could not quickly solve this pressing social problem and that some measure of government intervention would become necessary. The task was going to demand government money for the provision of housing, a revolutionary concept at the time, and guidelines had to be established particularly with regard to the question of building density. On March 18th 1918 the Local Government Board issued a circular to local authorities recommending a density of no more than twelve houses per acre for urban areas and eight per acre for rural areas. A Select Committee was appointed later in the same year under the chairmanship of Sir John Tudor Walters, MP and the recommendations of its report, published in 1918 and laboriously entitled: *Building Construction: Report of a Committee appointed to consider questions of Building Construction in connection with the Provision of Dwellings for the Working Class,* have remained the basis of the standards of accommodation to the present day. They included suggestions that three bedrooms should be the standard for family houses; there should provision for heating in all rooms; an inside lavatory and a bathroom. The Tudor Walter report also recommended that building components such as baths, windows and doors should be made to standard specifications; it proposed that building methods should be improved and that housing schemes should be prepared by competent architects. One of its more interesting recommendations was that no two-storey house should be less than seventy feet from its opposite neighbour and it calculated this figure by reference to the angle of the sun at noon in mid-winter. This standard of minimum distance, it reckoned, would ensure that the direct sunlight could always penetrate the ground-floor windows whatever the time of year.

In 1919 the Government produced its own *Housing Manual* which included most of the Tudor Walters recommendations, giving it official approval, and it was this manual that reinforced the three-bedroom, two-storey semi-detached house as the basis of most inter-war housing construction. 'Old Joe' Lister had been in so many ways ahead of his time for, although he may never have actually thought of it, the semi-detached house neatly solved the problem of access to the back-garden and the back-door. In terraces this can only be achieved by either going through the house, providing a back alley which is wasteful as far as land is concerned, or creating a tunnel through the block which necessitates neighbours using other people's gardens as rights of way, often leading to disputes. The semi-detached house was built in huge numbers in the inter-war years and Listerdale is but one example of its popularity. It was not overtaken as a model for housing provision until after the Second World War when multi-storey flats were for a time looked upon as the panacea for the housing shortage. Many such high-rise schemes had disastrous consequences and have since been demolished.

Dr Christopher Addison had become a Liberal Member of Parliament in 1910 and very soon became involved with David Lloyd George who asked him to help in seeing the National Insurance Bill through the Commons in 1911. When Lloyd George became Prime Minister in 1916 Addison was appointed Minister for Reconstruction and he set about drawing up a new plan for post-war Britain. Lloyd George may have been responsible for the policy of 'homes fit for heroes' but it fell to Addison to devise ways of implementing it. As Minister for Reconstruction he was very instrumental in establishing a new ministry, the Ministry of Health, becoming himself the first ever incumbent of that department in June, 1919, and using the Housing and Town Planning Act of that year, he drew up a blueprint for housing schemes. For the first time ever, there was to be a government subsidy for the building of houses and local authorities were encouraged to build low rent houses with any of the cost above a penny rate covered by Exchequer subsidy. Addison's scheme helped to establish local authorities as a major provider of rented housing in the inter-war years but, crucially for Joe Lister, the Addison subsidy also extended to private builders who were building houses for sale.

The Government's aim was to build 500,000 houses under this scheme which would have gone a very long way towards solving the crisis, but there was a severe economic slump in the winter of 1920/21 and Addison's expensive scheme came in for tremendous criticism. He was labelled a 'squandermaniac' by the press and the subsidies were abruptly withdrawn in July, 1921. Addison was forced to resign and lost his seat in the subsequent election of 1922. He deserted the Liberal party at that point and re-entered Parliament in 1929 as Labour MP for Swindon. He died in 1951 as 1st Viscount Addison. Joe Lister would always have reason to be grateful to him as, even though it may not have been apparent at the time, he would have had an even greater struggle to create Listerdale without the Exchequer subsidies. Addison's short-term measures proved to be a vital ingredient for Joe Lister's future enterprise on the edge of Rotherham. He may or may not have realised it at the time but he had every reason to be grateful to the first Minister of Health.

Government intervention in housing might have seemed curtailed with the departure of Addison from the Ministry of Health and the abrupt withdrawal of subsidies, but the problem would not go away and the Housing Act of 1923, introduced by Neville Chamberlain, who was appointed Minister of Health in the Conservative Government which succeeded, was intended to encourage private builders; this Act effectively made state subsidy an established part of house building in the inter-war years. The 1923 Act proved to be vitally important for the later development of Joe Lister's estate as its provisions went further than the 'Addison' measures. It made subsidies available to private house builders where the houses were to be built, not just for sale to owner-occupiers, but for letting, the only instance of a direct Exchequer subsidy to private landlords in the history of British housing. A short-lived Labour Government took over in 1924, the first Labour Government in British history, and extended this legislation under its Minister of Health, John Wheatley, the author of the 'Wheatley Act', under the terms of which most of the Listerdale houses were built. In 1927 the subsidy was reduced and in 1929 it was decided to phase it out in favour of subsidies to local authority housing alone in order to concentrate on slum clearance. However, these measures had provided golden opportunities for Joe and, as we have seen, he certainly took them.

SELECT BIBLIOGRAPHY

Mumford, Anthony P: *Rotherham, A Pictorial History,* Phillimore, 1994

Guest, John 1866: *Relics and Records*: re-published by Rotherham MBC, 1980

Greene, Dorothy FSA: *The Chapel of Our Lady on Rotherham Bridge*, Rotherham BC, 1951

Orbach, Laurence F: *Homes for Heroes*, Seeley Service & Co Ltd, 1977

Swenarton, Mark: *Homes Fit for Heroes*, Heinemann, 1981

Holmans, A: *Housing Policy in Britain*, Croom Helm, 1987

Edwards, Arthur M: *The Design of Suburbia*, Pembridge Press Ltd, 1981

Morris, Eleanor Smith: *British Town Planning and Urban Design*, Longman, 1997

Wilson, A N: *The Victorians*, Arrow Books, 2003

INDEX

Publications and page numbers of illustrations are shown in italics.

welfare of young people, 153-4, 156-8, 177; *see also*
    Rotherham & District Boys' Welfare Club
will, *see also* statement of affairs, 181-2
50th birthday, 167-9
60th birthday, 179
Lister, Joseph, father of 'Old Joe' Lister
    and grandfather of James, 9
Lister, Joyce, wife of Clifford, 134
Lister, Marjorie Greenhough, daughter of Joe, 54, 56, 62,
    74, 101-3, 106, 112-13, 151, *171*, 176-7, 179, 182, 183
Lister, Mary Evelyne, wife of Joe, 41, *42*, 43, 44, 45, 53,
    56, 58, 61, 63, 64, 74, 98, 99-101, 102, 126, 137
Lister, Megan, wife of Donald, 103-4
Lister, Minnie, 45
Lister, Myfanwy, *see* Megan Lister
Lister, 'Old Joe', grandfather of Joe, 2, 6-9, *7*, 11, 20, 23
Lister, Thomas Donald, *see* Donald Lister
Lister Castle, *see* Listerdale Estate
Listerdale Estate, 1, 2-4, 11, 12, 19, 66, 69, 72-4, 76, 81,
    82, 83, 84-6, 92, 94, 96-7, 150-1, 154-6, 175-6,
      182-5
  bathing pools, 83-4, *84*, 177
  Bawtry Road, 64, 76-80, *80*, 81, 128, 150
  Black Carr Road, 95, *95*, 110, 149
  Brecks Crescent, 96, 110
  Brecks Farm, 59, 92
  Brecks Lane, 58, 92, 94, 115
  building for rent, 91-2, 93, 95-96, 108-10, 114, 115-16;
    see also rented properties
  building subsidies, 66-7, 68, 73-4, 77, 87-9, 92-4, 95,
    97, 107, 108-9, 114-15, 176
  Castle House, *see* The Castle
  community facilities, 152; hall,153-4, 167
  Dale Road, 98
  donations of land, 153
  Estate Foreman, 179, 183, 184
  Estate Hall, *see* community facilities
  Estate Office, 133
  Estate shop, 150-1

Milton, Lord, *see* Lord Fitzwilliam
Moat Farm, Wickersley, 170, 174, 179, 183
Mond, Sir Alfred, 66
Motor, 138, 146

'Old Listerdale', *see* Listerdale Estate
owner-occupiers, *see* Listerdale Estate
Oxley & Coward, solicitors, 69, 70-2, 86, 87-8, 92, 96, 168,
    169, 179

Parish Church of Sheffield, *see* Sheffield Cathedral
Pax Britannica, 22
Peabody, George, 154
   The Peabody Trust, 154-5
Pickles, Arthur, 71-2, 96, 168, 169
Pierson, Harold, 43, 45, 52
Poor Law Amendment Act 1834, 17
Port Sunlight, 12
Powell, Annie, 104
Princip, Gavrilo, 47
Property owners, *see* Tenants
psittacosis, 100-1

Ranskill, recreational facilities, 124
rented properties, *see* Listerdale Estate
Richard I, (The Lionheart), 118
River Don, 24, 159
River Rother, 23
road improvements, 77-80, *80*
Robson, Jock, 113
Roddis, W H, 74
Rodreham, now Rotherham, 23
Rother Vale Collieries Company Ltd, 10
Rother Valley Tramways Committee, 77-8
Rotherham, 1, 2, 4, 6-7, 22, 23-7, 31
    Alma House, 154
    All Saints Parish Church, 13, 23
    Brecks Hotel, 58, 92
    Chantry Chapel of Our Lady, 23